A NEWMARKET PICTO[...]

Evan Seth McLovin

SUPERBAD
The Illustrated Moviebook

With the Complete Screenplay Written by SETH ROGEN & EVAN GOLDBERG

Introduction by JUDD APATOW

Drawings by DAVID GOLDBERG

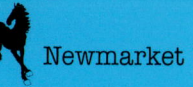

Newmarket Press • New York

Copyright © 2007 Columbia Pictures Industries, Inc. All rights reserved.

Seth's drawings by David Goldberg

Permission acknowledgments can be found on page 144.

The Newmarket Shooting Script® Series is a registered trademark of Newmarket Publishing & Communications Company.

This book is published simultaneously in the United States of America and in Canada. All rights reserved. This book may not be reproduced, in whole or in part, in any form, without written permission. Inquiries should be addressed to: Permissions Department, Newmarket Press, 18 East 48th Street, New York, NY 10017.

FIRST EDITION

10 9 8 7 6 5 4 3 2 1

ISBN: 978-1-55704-798-4

Library of Congress Catalog-in-Publication Data available upon request.

Quantity Purchases

Companies, professional groups, clubs, and other organizations may qualify for special terms when ordering quantities of this title. For information, write to Special Sales, Newmarket Press, 18 East 48th Street, New York, NY 10017; call (212) 832-3575 or 1-800-669-3903; FAX (212) 832-3629; or e-mail info@newmarketpress.com. Website: www.newmarketpress.com

Manufactured in the United States of America.

The Newmarket Shooting Script® Series Includes:

About a Boy: The Shooting Script
Adaptation: The Shooting Script
The Age of Innocence: The Shooting Script
American Beauty: The Shooting Script
A Beautiful Mind: The Shooting Script
Big Fish: The Shooting Script
The Birdcage: The Shooting Script
Black Hawk Down: The Shooting Script
Capote: The Shooting Script
Cast Away: The Shooting Script
Cinderella Man: The Shooting Script
The Constant Gardener: The Shooting Script
Dead Man Walking: The Shooting Script
Eternal Sunshine of the Spotless Mind: The Shooting Script
Gods and Monsters: The Shooting Script
The Good Shepherd: The Shooting Script
Gosford Park: The Shooting Script
Human Nature: The Shooting Script
The Ice Storm: The Shooting Script
In Good Company: The Shooting Script
Knocked Up: The Shooting Script
Little Miss Sunshine: The Shooting Script
Little Children: The Shooting Script
Man on the Moon: The Shooting Script
The Matrix: The Shooting Script
Michael Clayton: The Shooting Script
The People vs. Larry Flynt: The Shooting Script
Pieces of April: The Shooting Script
Punch-Drunk Love: The Shooting Script
Sense and Sensibility: The Shooting Script
The Shawshank Redemption: The Shooting Script
Sideways: The Shooting Script
The Squid and the Whale: The Shooting Script
Stranger Than Fiction: The Shooting Script
Traffic: The Shooting Script
Thank You for Smoking: The Shooting Script
Transamerica: The Shooting Script
United 93: The Shooting Script
War of the Worlds: The Shooting Script

Other Newmarket Pictorial Moviebooks and Newmarket Insider Film Books Include:

The Art of The Matrix*
The Art of X2*
The Art of X-Men: The Last Stand
Bram Stoker's Dracula: The Film and the Legend*
Chicago: The Movie and Lyrics*
Dances with Wolves: The Illustrated Story of the Epic Film*
Dreamgirls
E.T. The Extra-Terrestrial: From Concept to Classic*
Gladiator: The Making of the Ridley Scott Epic Film
Good Night, and Good Luck: The Screenplay and History Behind the Landmark Movie*
A Good Year: Portrait of the Film
Hitchhiker's Guide to the Galaxy: The Filming of the Douglas Adams Classic
Hotel Rwanda: Bringing the True Story of an African Hero to Film*
The Jaws Log
Kinsey: Public and Private*
Memoirs of a Geisha: A Portrait of the Film
Ray: A Tribute to the Movie, the Music, and the Man*
Saving Private Ryan: The Men, The Mission, The Movie
Schindler's List: Images of the Steven Spielberg Film
Tim Burton's Corpse Bride: An Invitation to the Wedding

*Includes screenplay.

Contents

INTRODUCTION by Judd Apatow 5

MEET SETH ROGEN AND EVAN GOLDBERG 8

CAST OF CHARACTERS 12

COMMENTARIES... Seriously!

"THE BOYS OF SUMMER" by David Edelstein 23

SUPERBAD by Peter Travers 26

"IT'S, LIKE, A BUDDY FILM BY, LIKE, BUDDIES" by Michael Cieply 29

"TALKIN' SUPERBAD: COMEDY ISN'T PRETTY" by Josh Rottenberg 33

MR. VAGTASTIC'S GUIDE TO BUYING PORN 48

THE PENIS GALLERY 53

THE SHOOTING SCRIPT 61

CAST AND CREW CREDITS 135

ABOUT THE FILMMAKERS 142

Introduction

by Judd Apatow

Superbad is the script that started it all. Long before there was a script for *The 40-Year-Old Virgin* or *Knocked Up*, there was *Superbad*. People often ask where the inspiration came from to make these frank R-rated movies, and the answer is *Superbad*.

Seth showed it to me in the year 2000 when we were shooting one of our many short-lived TV series, *Undeclared*. At the time he was eighteen years old. He told me that he started writing it when he was fourteen with his partner and best friend, Evan Goldberg, who was then thirteen. Their inspiration was a hatred of teen movies and the belief that even kids who had just grown pubic hair that very year could do better. It is pretty astounding that what they wrote was funny. There is no reason why it should be funny. All logic would point to it being a piece of crap, irritating, mindless, and illogical, but it was not. It makes you want to smack them.

The draft I saw, which was already four years in the making, was one of the funniest scripts I had ever read. It lacked in a few areas, but laughs were not one of them. They had created some classic characters. Sure, the characters were based on themselves and their friends, but aren't all characters based on someone you know? It also had dick drawings, and lots of them. And a set piece centered around menstrual blood. They told me they wanted to write the movie they wished someone would make. They said that if anyone ever dared to make this movie, all their friends would go nuts for it and it would be a big hit. It is not often that young men who spend so much time smoking pot out of a fishbowl can be so clear about their vision of the future, but this was one of those times.

It took a long time to convince anyone that this movie should be made. From the start I thought it would get made, but I never thought it would take another seven years. This project took four years longer to birth than *Gandhi*, and that took ten years. Initially some people were interested, but thought the menstrual blood scene had to go and that the film had no hook

Superbad

for marketing. Changes were made, hope was in the air, but it led nowhere. We were willing to make it for the lowest budget imaginable, but we could not even get that. After *Anchorman* was a hit, I thought now *Superbad* would have its day. Hollywood said up yours. After *The 40-Year-Old Virgin*, I thought we would have the leverage to make *Superbad*, but Hollywood said go fuck yourself.

Finally, after *Talladega Nights* succeeded at the box office for Sony Pictures, we had finally gotten to a place where a studio believed we should be allowed to make *Superbad*. They actually thought it was funny and were enthusiastic about giving us $20 million to make it. It was shocking.

In all the years we waited, Seth and Evan continued to punch up the script. It got better and better. Like a fine wine, *Superbad* matured into the cock-filled, sweet-natured filthfest it now is. It found its heart and then its stars: Jonah Hill, Michael Cera, and Christopher Mintz-Plasse. Sure, Seth Rogen was now too old to be the star of the film he wrote for himself, but one mustache and a gun later and he and Bill Hader are the most badass cops one could ever have wished for.

I am so proud of this film. I like what it says and I laugh my ass off at how it says it. I am amazed that I stuck with it for so long. It seems kind of insane now. And I stand in awe of Seth and Evan's writing. It is insightful, reckless, genuinely good-hearted, and hysterical. And it only took fourteen years. Over half of their lives went into the making of this film. Actually, now that I think about it too much, it is kind of sad. ■

Seth Rogen (left) and Judd Apatow at the premiere.

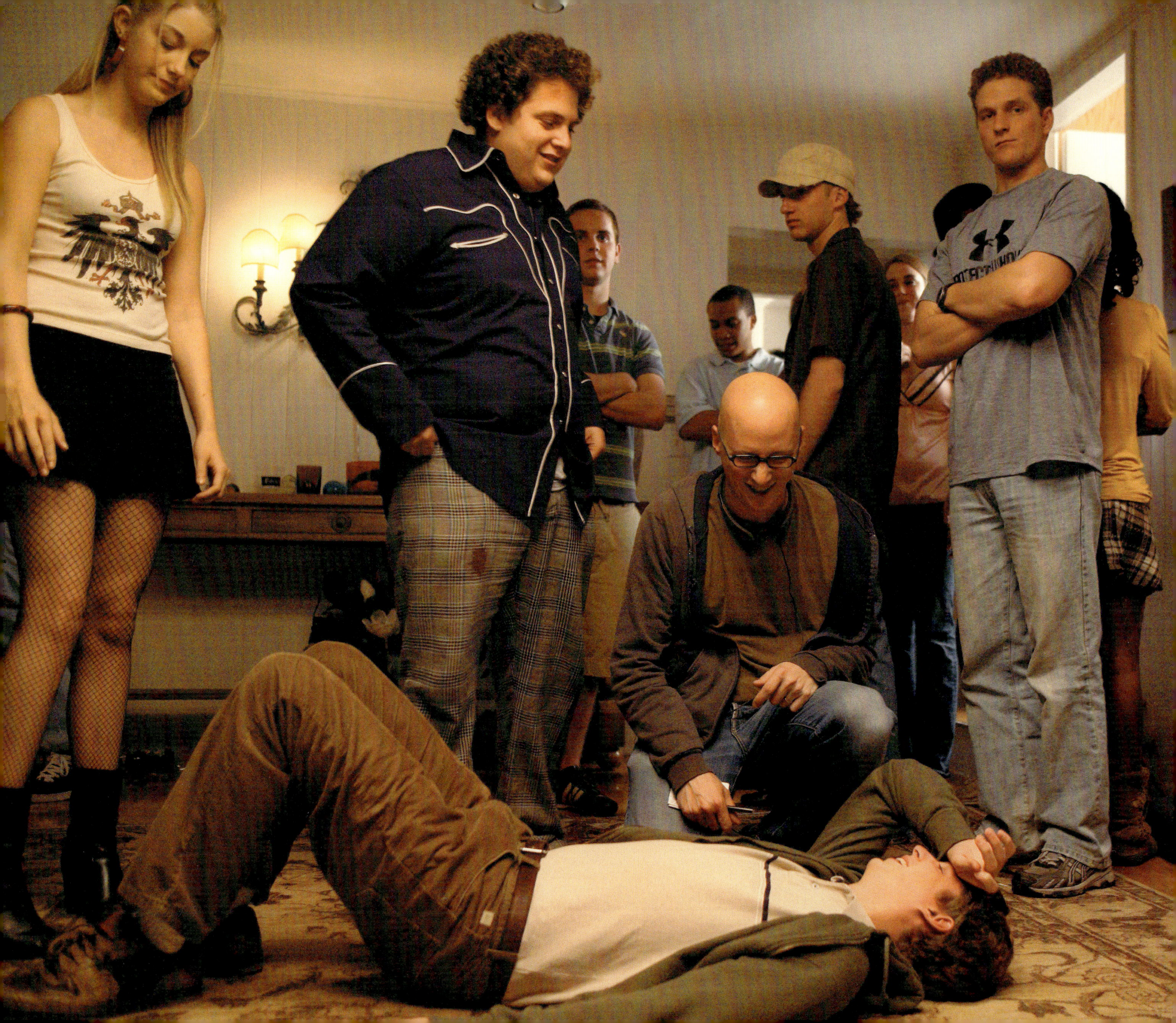

Meet Evan Goldberg

and Seth Rogen

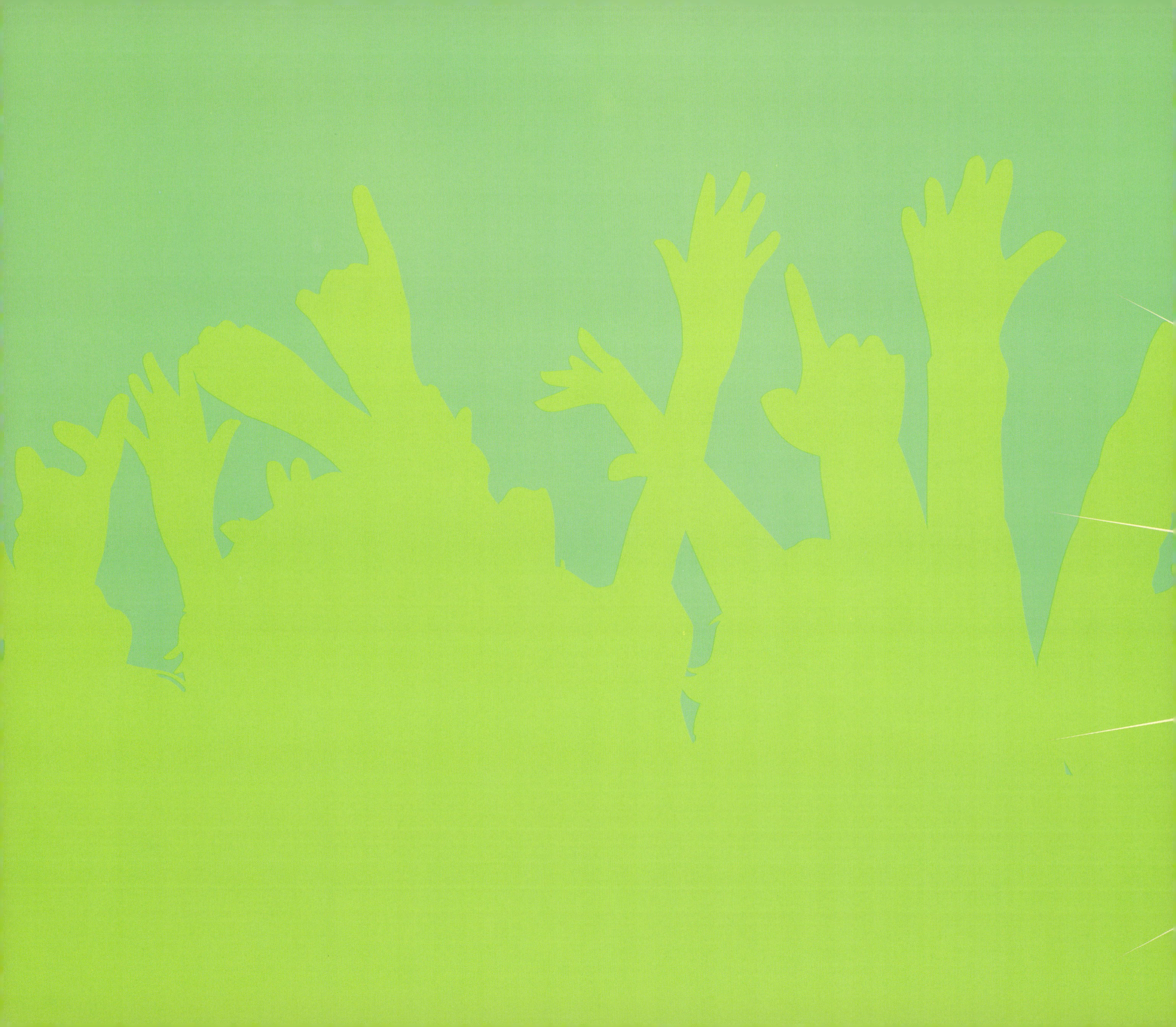

Cast of Characters

Superbad

"It's one of those crazy Hollywood stories that you hear sometimes. You think stuff like that just doesn't happen and then it happens. I'm lucky."

—Seth, Jonah Hill

The search was both exhaustive and exhausting for Seth. "I was getting really frustrated," says Producer Judd Apatow. Then, inspiration struck when Apatow looked around at those closest to him. "At that time I was directing *Knocked Up*, another film in which Jonah Hill was acting. I was walking with Seth and looked over at Jonah and said, 'I guess Jonah will do it.'"

The writers Seth Rogen and Evan Goldberg did not respond kindly to the suggestion at first.

"I was like, 'Like hell it's Jonah,'" says Goldberg. "'He looks 27. You're all crazy. You've all lost your minds.'"

Rogen adds dryly, "Jonah was our dead last choice."

Producer Shauna Robertson explains, "Jonah was just someone we forgot to consider because I don't like to admit that he's that young. He's one of my wisest friends, so I keep forgetting that he's not a 43-year-old man."

Hill says, "Judd just looked at me and asked, 'How young can you play?' I said, 'I don't know. 17 or something.' And then he asked me if I wanted to play the lead in *Superbad*." On the spur of the moment, the actor shot a videotape of himself in the role of Seth. Apatow sent the tape to Director Greg Mottola and the chairman of the studio, and that was that. He had the part.

Seth

Jonah Hill

Evan

Michael Cera

cast of characters

"We did a lot of rehearsals and read-throughs before shooting, Jonah and I hung out a lot. It's kind of funny the way they were trying to plan these hang-out dates for us, when we were already hanging out."
—Evan, Michael Cera

came up with a brilliant idea. "We wanted to force them to spend as much time as possible together," recalls Robertson. "Judd said to me very early on, 'Maybe we should make them live in the same apartment together!'" After all, this is a group that is well known for working with their own friends. Robertson explains, "We mostly make these movies to put our friends in awkward situations."

Casting Evan was a much easier task. "I'd directed a couple of episodes of 'Arrested Development,' and was a big fan of Michael Cera," says Mottola. "I'd seen what he was capable of. That show was filled with a lot of funny, talented people, and Michael completely held his own—sometimes, he was the best in the room."

Mottola adds that Cera and Hill make a perfect combination: "Michael makes being sweet and dorky incredibly hilarious. Jonah makes being a vulgar loudmouth into something really kind of sweet."

Cera was the first actor cast and when Jonah fell into the mix, the filmmakers, unaware that the two already knew each other socially, and wanting to make sure they had chemistry,

15

Superbad

"My friend found out about the casting call and said, 'You look like you could fit the part, you should come down with us.' It was my first audition, my first acting role—the first anything I've ever done."
—McLovin, Christopher Mintz-Plasse

Then, towards the end of the day, came Christopher Mintz-Plasse. "Chris was one of the last ones we saw. I remember him leaving the room and Alison and I looking at each other, thinking, 'That can't be as good as it seems, can it?'" says Mottola. "Chris was the first person to play him as the arrogant nerd—the guy who thinks he's Frank Sinatra, even though he looks like Truman Capote. It was hilarious."

"Chris is one of those wonderful little miracles," says Apatow. "You're looking for a hilarious young person, someone hears about your movie, comes in for a short audition and is instantly great; during the shoot, he gets even better than you ever hoped he could have been."

"I've worked with just about everybody in the cast before except for Chris," adds Robertson. "Chris came into that atmosphere, where everything is very free and loose, and he just knocked it out of the park."

McLovin
Christopher Mintz-Plasse

Officer Slater
Bill Hader

Officer Michaels
Seth Rogen

cast of characters

Becca
Martha MacIsaac

Jules
Emma Stone

19

Comme

taries
...Seriously!

Superbad

The Boys of Summer

by David Edelstein

From *New York* magazine, August 27, 2007

Superbad might be the most provocative teen sex comedy ever made; it is certainly one of the most convulsively funny. Its protagonists are graduating high-school buddies swimming in hormones and uncertainty. Seth (Jonah Hill) is blobby and loud; Evan (Michael Cera) skinny, hysterical, and a tad girlish. (Think Mostel and Wilder in *The Producers*.) A virgin and likely to remain so for some time, Seth talks of nothing but sex—a nonstop stream of F- and P- and D-words that would make David Mamet sit up and salute. The more prepossessing Evan is embarrassed by his friend's sexist ejaculations; he respects women—from afar. (He shifts and stammers around the cute female classmate flashing him the tongue.) Both look to a party that evening for resolution. Their task is to procure alcohol, which Seth is sure will get them laid. In the course of their odyssey, they plunge into a night world of sex, drugs, and aggression in which no one's development is unarrested.

The co-producer is Judd Apatow, of *Knocked Up*, the co-writer Seth Rogen of the same. Some right-wing commentators pretzeled themselves up to praise that film—which had naughty words and drugs and premarital sex but, hallelujah, came down squarely on the side of family values. The same is true of *Superbad*, but the pretzels will have to be even twistier. Apatow and company (the director here is Greg Mottola) have a pipeline to the adolescent id and a little too much fun frolicking in its hot springs of obscenity. If teens come away with the message that booze and sex and drugs can't buy them love (or happiness), they'll also feel the compulsion to talk dirty, drink, fuck, and learn the lesson for themselves—as well they should, provided they don't kill themselves doing it.

Superbad is like *American Graffiti*, with a crucial difference: The adults are as childlike and out of control as the children (if not more so). In George Lucas's funny-sad paean to lost innocence, the teens sabotaged a police cruiser; in *Superbad*, two drunken cops (Rogen and Bill Hader, a master of deadpan dementia) shoot up their own car to impress Seth and Evan's dorky friend, Fogell (Christopher Mintz-Plasse). Dispatched to buy the booze, Fogell has created a fake I.D. bearing the one-word pseudonym "McLovin"—a name that will live, I predict, as long as teen movies. He's so endearingly not a McLovin that you can almost understand the policemen's infatuation with him. He is the primordial, Jungian dork within us all.

Superbad

By the time the cops are firing guns in juvenile ecstasy, the movie has entered a fugue state. Adam Sternbergh in this magazine called those unable to let go of childhood "grups," while writer Christopher Noxon has dubbed them "rejuveniles": Whatever you call them, Apatow has become their Florenz Ziegfeld—and maybe, too, their David Lynch. Still in search of alcohol, Seth and Evan stumble into a grown-up inferno in which hairy men inexplicably punch one another to a pulp. An addled redneck cokehead makes Evan sing for him, while a busty babe who dirty-dances with the enraptured Seth leaves his trousers smeared with menstrual blood. It's like the "candy-colored clown they call the sandman" sequence in *Blue Velvet*. The donkey scene in *Pinocchio* also comes to mind. This is where delinquents go to degenerate.

At close to two hours, *Superbad* feels fifteen minutes too long, although Mottola and writers Rogen and Evan Goldberg want to take you past the high to the inevitable plummet. No *American Pie* climactic couplings here. Instead: puke and loathing. The filmmakers linger on the homoerotic undercurrents of adolescent male friendship in a way that other teen sex comedies avoid like the (gay) plague. That's what makes *Superbad* so vital—and so of its time. In the seventies and eighties, even explicit teen sex comedies like *Fast Times at Ridgemont High* unfolded in a culture with a fair amount of shame. Now, with *Fast Times* and *American Pie* as touchstones, with MySpace turning even shy people into exhibitionists, filmmakers can begin where their predecessors ended. Soon it might not be repression we have to worry about but having nothing left to repress. ■

commentaries... seriously!

Superbad

by Peter Travers

From *Rolling Stone* magazine, August 7, 2007

The geek boy has been a staple of comedy since the Greeks. OK, I'm lying, but you know what I mean. He's the scrawny dickhead with no chance of ever getting laid. Except in the movies, that is. Now, as McLovin in *Superbad*, Christopher Mintz-Plasse (hardly a name you expect to see up in lights) reinvents the geek boy for the new century. He's a big reason why the hip, hot and hilarious *Superbad* packs more gut-busting laughs than you can count. Judd Apatow produced this raunchy antidote to *High School Musical* from a script that Apatow's *Knocked Up* star Seth Rogen wrote with his Canadian school chum Evan Goldberg when they were—do you effing believe this?—thirteen.

This deceptively throwaway farce (it's actually a keeper that comes up aces in writing, acting and directing) takes place entirely on one night, when three high school losers desperately try to hustle booze for a party in the illusory hope that hotties will be more likely to give them head. Chubby Seth (Jonah Hill) and dorky Evan (Michael Cera) leave the task of obtaining fake ID to Fogell, a four-eyed creature from the nerd lagoon who instills confidence in no one but himself. He creates a driver's license that cites his age as twenty-five, his address as Hawaii and his name (just one) as McLovin. What should fool no one instead bedazzles all, including two cops, played by *SNL*'s Bill Hader and Rogen (his riff on guns and cocks is classic). McLovin—the license ID's him as an organ donor—is suddenly cool.

And Mintz-Plasse, who has never acted before (hell, he's in high school), makes McLovin a geek icon for the ages. Long after you've forgotten a decade of Oscar winners, you'll remember McLovin. Mintz-Plasse knocks it out of the park.

commentaries... Seriously!

More good news: *Superbad* is superfun across the board. Apatow has nurtured the script ever since Rogen used it as a calling card to get TV work as an actor and writer on Apatow's *Freaks and Geeks* and *Undeclared*. Sadly, Rogen was deemed too old (at twenty-five) to play himself as a teen. So the role of Seth fell to Hill, Rogen's co-star in *The 40-Year-Old Virgin*, who is only one year younger. Irony—you gotta love it. With *Arrested Development*'s Cera, 19, playing Evan, *Superbad* had its buddies in place and a director, Greg Mottola (*The Daytrippers*), with the style and smarts to bring it home.

It helps that the fun doesn't stop. It helps even more that the pitch-perfect script doesn't step out of character for a joke. Chunky vomit, menstrual blood and artful penis drawings are all part of the growth process. Rogen and Goldberg know how horny adolescents talk. Evan, doing a deep think on why a girl's nipples can make his dick go boing, wishes babes could feel the same way about his erections. Don't we all. And beneath the teasing banter—with an added dollop of queer fear—Hill and Cera deftly uncover two scared teens trying to hide their feelings. Seth worries that Evan will go to Dartmouth and punk out on their friendship, leaving him to grow up like the two cops—lost boys with badges, played with crazed zeal and surprising nuance by Hader and Rogen. Powered by a comedy dream team, this shitfaced *American Graffiti* dares to show it has a heart. So step up for *Superbad*, and find your inner McLovin. ∎

Superbad

commentaries... seriously!

It's, Like, a Buddy Film by, Like, Buddies

by Michael Cieply

From *New York Times*, August 5, 2007

Seth Rogen really does look that way. In life the fuzzy-headed nebbish from *Knocked Up* is, well, a fuzzy-headed nebbish, though these days he appears a little trimmer—is somebody training for next year's *Green Hornet*?—than when he hooked up with Katherine Heigl in the hit movie. (Mr. Rogen recently agreed to help write and possibly star in *Green Hornet*, Columbia's planned movie about the comic-book hero.)

His writing partner, Evan Goldberg, does not customarily appear on screen. But Mr. Goldberg could pass for one of the rumpled man-boy characters in the comedies, directed by Judd Apatow, that Mr. Rogen has helped populate of late. Over something between breakfast and lunch last month at the Los Angeles diner Swingers, Mr. Goldberg, 24, and Mr. Rogen, 25, talked with Michael Cieply about the raunchy movie *Superbad*, which they started writing 12 years ago, when they were growing up in Vancouver, British Columbia.

Superbad was directed by Greg Mottola (*The Daytrippers*). It stars Michael Cera and Jonah Hill as not even thinly disguised versions of the writers, doing what kids have done in *Fast Times at Ridgemont High* and other predecessors. That is, they spend a day trying to get loaded, get lucky with the opposite sex, and generally avoid the implications of a looming semi-adult life. In *Superbad* the actual plot, such as it is, has to do with buying alcohol for a cool girls' party, with the help of a fake ID, which eventually lands a buddy named Fogell in the company of some cops (one played by Mr. Rogen) with issues of their own.

Q. *What kind of people spend half their lives writing a script they start at 13?*

ROGEN: It's sad when you put it like that, I guess. Young ones.
GOLDBERG: We didn't do it with great thought, we just did it. We didn't have anything to do.

Q. *What did you think you were going to do with it?*

GOLDBERG: In our heads we were like, oh, we'll get this made. I think we thought were going to get it done by the time we were 30.

ROGEN: The thing about Vancouver, it's very far away from Hollywood, but they make things there. It's not like growing up in Tallahassee and writing a thing where really there is no chance it will ever get seen by anyone. It just didn't seem like it would happen any time soon.

Q. *Do you think it's possible to do an authentic movie about teenagers that they're not rated out of unless they bring their parents?*

ROGEN: There's a movie we made with Owen Wilson, called *Drillbit Taylor*. It's rated PG-13, but the kids in it are 14 years old, and we were like pushing it. But I feel like once you're 15 and 16, and people start driving and you get way more freedom and independence and then all of a sudden you're alone with people and you can party and stuff.

Q. *How come there are so many funny Canadians?*

ROGEN: I think it's because we grow up with all of the same stuff a lot of Americans grow up with, but we just are kind of taught to look at it a little differently. The one thing you're aware of in Canada is that you're not American. But you only know that because everything you get is from America. The TV's American. All the movies are American. So you're just kind of imbued to look at it, I don't know if critically is the right word, just kind of differently.

GOLDBERG: Like, I went to Taco Bell, and the security guard had a gun. I thought I should leave. I thought, is he a security guard? Is he a robber?

ROGEN: Exactly. They say going to Israel is crazy because everyone has a machine gun. It's really not that different from here when every security guard has a large weapon in the parking lot of the grocery store.

GOLDBERG: Every Canadian just cannot believe the portions of food.

ROGEN: Oh, yeah, that's another thing.

GOLDBERG: It's the most astounding thing, it's just double. It's double what you should get.

Q. *Is there a real Fogell?*

GOLDBERG: Yeah, he was actually our best friend.

ROGEN: Still is our best friend.

GOLDBERG: Sammy Fogell. He's coming down here for the premiere. I was just up in Vancouver hanging out with him.

ROGEN: It's funny because Fogell's a name we use in several scripts, because it's a name we like.

GOLDBERG: Actually we wanted to use it in every script.

Q. *Is there anything about the characters in* Superbad *that is not based on you two?*

ROGEN: We never really had any emotional issues, ever, throughout our entire time knowing each other.

GOLDBERG: We've never hugged.

commentaries... Seriously!

Q. *Does* Superbad *bring something new to the teenage comedy genre?*

ROGEN: It might be new for this generation, I guess.
GOLDBERG: It's kind of a callback.
ROGEN: I bet when *Fast Times* came out, it was exactly what we hoped to do, which was make something that people would say this is how we actually are. What other good high school movies are there?

Q. American Graffiti?

ROGEN: Exactly.
GOLDBERG: It's on my Netflix, I haven't seen it.

Q. *The boys in your movie are slower. In* American Graffiti *Ron Howard is going off to college and trying to break up with his girlfriend. In* Superbad *they're going to college and still trying to get a girl.*

ROGEN: That was just us.
GOLDBERG: All that says is that Ron Howard was cooler than we were. ∎

Superbad

Talkin' Superbad: Comedy Isn't Pretty

by Josh Rottenberg

From *Entertainment Weekly*, August 17, 2007

As the old Joni Mitchell song goes, Judd Apatow has looked at life from both sides now. Before tasting the thrill of victory—as the producer of hit comedies like *Anchorman* and *Talladega Nights* and the director of 2005's *The 40-Year-Old Virgin* and this summer's *Knocked Up*—he experienced the agony of defeat as the creator of such brilliant-but-cancelled TV series as *The Ben Stiller Show*, *Freaks and Geeks*, and *Undeclared*. Victory, it's safe to say, is a lot more fun. With the latest film from the white-hot Apatow laugh factory, the raunchy high school comedy *Superbad*, we brought together Apatow (the film's producer), Seth Rogen (its cowriter and costar), and the film's two leads, Jonah Hill and Michael Cera, for a rollicking and very R-rated conversation about the ins and outs of comedy—the supergood, the superbad, and the superugly.

Q. **ENTERTAINMENT WEEKLY:** *Why do you think these movies are clicking now? You've been on the critically beloved but under-seen side of things. What's different now?*

JUDD APATOW: Well, you know, sometimes I think maybe people just didn't like *Freaks and Geeks* and sometimes I think it was just all scheduling and marketing. Now I think it was definitely scheduling and marketing.

SETH ROGEN: We've proven that.

JONAH HILL: [To Apatow] Did you ever really think that people didn't like it?

APATOW: I thought maybe there were less people that liked that kind of thing than I had thought. I thought people would be so happy to have a show that was funny, sort of honest, and about geeks and potheads. It just seemed like something that could be really popular.

Q. *It should at least have beaten season 10 of* Cops.

APATOW: I remember I always used to say to Paul Feig, "If we can't beat the 10th season of *Cops*, we shouldn't be on the air." And we didn't. Whenever you get bad ratings, there's always an excuse that everyone makes. The first episode got huge ratings, and then the second episode just ate it. It really dropped.

And everyone said, "Well, it's because the lead-in was different. Your lead-in this week was *The Tejano Heritage Awards*. Next week it'll be different." And then it didn't go up and then they moved us, and then right after they moved us, ABC moved the Regis *Who Wants to Be a Millionaire* show against us, and we just said, "OK, it's over."
ROGEN: I was on *Regis* yesterday. I should have told him that he cancelled us.
APATOW: He destroyed us. How was Regis?
ROGEN: He was awesome. He called me Josh by accident. I saw him in the hall and he said, "Hey, Josh!" I was like, That was weird, but I let it slide.
APATOW: Who did he think you were, Josh Hartnett?
ROGEN: I don't know. But he's so nice. I totally thought, if he's a d---, that's fine with me. He's been on TV forever, he's f---ing Regis—he's allowed to be an a--hole. But he was really, really nice.
APATOW: I met him once and he was so hilarious. He's like what you wish your family was like.
ROGEN: Except talking to him and Kelly Ripa, I kept feeling like I was talking to someone's grandpa and his trophy wife.
APATOW: Whose grandpa?
ROGEN: Michael Cera's.
APATOW: Did I answer any aspect of your question?

Q. *You blamed everything on Fox, Regis, and the Tejanos.*

APATOW: Well, you know, when *Freaks and Geeks* got cancelled, we thought, Wouldn't it be great if we got picked up by Showtime and we could do the cursing, really frank version, where you saw them smoke pot and you saw how messed up they really were? And then Showtime never called.
MICHAEL CERA: Same thing with *Arrested Development*. One of the writers, Jim Vallely, said if we got picked up on Showtime, the first shot he would want of season 4 of *Arrested Development* would be a shot of Will Arnett having sex with a girl from behind. Just to kick it off.

Q. *So it doesn't seem like there's been any shift in audience's tastes in your direction?*

APATOW: A change in America? I don't think so at all, other than they allowed us to make a couple of movies and before they didn't allow us to make any movies. These are the same movies that have been rejected for the last half-decade.
ROGEN: The people who didn't make *Superbad* the last 10 years will probably claim the audience's tastes have shifted, but I don't think they have.
HILL: *[To Apatow]* So why did they let you make *40-Year-Old Virgin*? Was it because of *Anchorman*?
APATOW: Yes, after we did *Anchorman*, it seemed clear that Steve Carell was awesome every day and could handle a starring role. And so it was a little easier to get that made. I think *Elf* also opened the door in a big way, because that and *Old School* seemed to get people excited about Will Ferrell and the people in Will's world. But I don't think anything's changed.

ROGEN: It's funny, I'm noticing when you do a lot of interviews, often the reporters go in with something they want you to say and they'll keep asking questions until you say it. And the two things that people seem to want us to say more than anything is that audience's tastes have changed and that we are all unconventional guys to be in comedies—both of which I very strongly disagree with.

APATOW: Don't they remember Jack Klugman?

ROGEN: Exactly!

APATOW: I always talk about Jack Klugman. In fact, when I was trying to get "unconventional" kids on *Freaks and Geeks*—that's a code word I use—

ROGEN: —for Jewish. *[Laughs]* "There are too many goddamn unconventionals at this country club!"

APATOW: "I've got to go to temple with my unconventional friends." But I always talked about Jack Klugman. Like, if you looked at all the great old television comedy, it was always Jack Klugman and Tony Randall and Phil Silvers.

ROGEN: We're the new Phil Silvers, Jack Klugman, and Tony Randall!

APATOW: I don't know when it became that people thought funny people were all so handsome. That's just an idea that I've always rejected. But what happens is that when people become popular, then people think they're sexy also for some reason.

HILL: Thank God. Well, I think it's funny because every interview they say, "You guys are leading men now and you're so unconventional," or whatever the hell the word is—

CERA: Untraditional.

HILL: And I go, like, "Do you guys think Will Ferrell and Jack Black look different from us? Those guys are big movie stars!"

ROGEN: If every comedy star is unconventional, doesn't that then become conventional?

APATOW: Do you guys get insulted by that?

ROGEN: No, I honestly just think they're crazy. It makes me feel like they've never heard of Albert Brooks or Woody Allen or W. C. Fields or the Marx Brothers or any other comedian.

HILL: They're acting like we're making movies like *Bourne Ultimatum*. It's not like we're in like f---ing *Ocean's 11* or something like that. We're making comedies!

ROGEN: It's a weird stance to take.

HILL: And it's everybody's stance.

APATOW: I never even thought that was one of the main jokes of *Knocked Up*. I didn't think it was that Katherine Heigl would be horrified at the sight of Seth. Because I think we're all cute.

ROGEN: I think we're fine.

APATOW: I think we're adorable.

HILL: And what's funny is that all of us date women that are far more attractive than we are. I feel like we're funny or likable and so that's what life is like. My whole life I've dated women that were considerably more attractive than I was comparatively.

CERA: Yeah, if you stood me in line with all my ex-girlfriends and said who's more attractive, it's always them.

APATOW: How long a line is that?

CERA: I don't know, maybe four feet.

ROGEN: If they lie down and lay head to toe?

APATOW: Or just one four-foot-long girl? *[Laughs]* I thought the joke of *Knocked Up* was that it was a guy that, after he slept with her, would talk about how much he loved smoking pot and how it was better than Tylenol. I didn't think it

Superbad

was a visual joke. Although I think when I first indicated to my wife [actress Leslie Mann] that I had interests beyond being friends, I don't know if she was thrilled about it.

Q. *The other thing that sets the Apatow-brand comedies apart is the combination of the hard-R kind of raunchiness with the emotional sweetness.*

APATOW: D--- and heart. That's what I'm going to call my new production company: D--- Heart Productions.

CERA: Those are the two key organs involved in life.

APATOW: There are obviously great comedies that aren't R-rated, but you can certainly do a very honest, frank, sweet, and also disgusting type of comedy with an R rating. I always enjoyed writing for *The Larry Sanders Show* because it was fun to hear Rip Torn say f---. To me, it's just about showing how people really express themselves. I mean, this conversation is R.

CERA: It was never a conscious effort to swear on *Superbad*. If anything, when we were doing the clean version for TV, it was a conscious effort *not* to swear.

APATOW: It was so hard to get Jonah to stop saying f---. We spent so much time trying to

commentaries... seriously!

thin out the f---s. It was like, "What f--- is not connected to a joke?"

HILL: One time Judd sent me an e-mail during shooting: "You should try not to curse so much, because you need to make it emphasize more when you do curse." I just wrote back: "F--- that."

APATOW: You've got the f--- crutch.

ROGEN: But if you're going to make a realistic movie, if the characters are over 15, it has to be R-rated.

HILL: Michael and I talked about how it never seems gratuitous.

ROGEN: To your mother it might.

HILL: It just seems like how people talk. If I got hit by a car, I'd be like, "F---!" It just seemed to me like it just sounded realistic.

APATOW: We got to a good f--- level.

ROGEN: We found our stride, f----wise.

HILL: Then I switched on the *vag*.

APATOW: I thought that when we showed *Superbad* to audiences, we would start an ongoing debate about how dirty should the movie be. And at the very first screening, nobody in the audience had any issue with anything in the movie in the numbers that would make you change it. I couldn't believe it. I thought we would be debating so many set pieces and language and cutting things. And there was nothing.

ROGEN: We didn't get to do anything to offend a large part of the audience. And we almost tried. It's pretty shocking.

CERA: So what's the biggest thing you guys have had to cut from your movies?

APATOW: On *Knocked Up*, we had to cut some jokes that made everyone dislike the friends. There was a run where they were talking about nude scenes and somebody was saying that they were going to view all of Julianne Moore's movies to catalog her nude scenes and that it was going to take them a couple of days.

HILL: I said her bush was like the hedge maze in *The Shining*.

ROGEN: And I went, "Red bush! Red bush!"

APATOW: And the whole audience got very upset.

ROGEN: And to me that was like a miraculous moment of genius!

HILL: I remember it ended and Seth and I high-fived. We were so proud of ourselves.

APATOW: It'll go back in on the DVD. There was a sequence we had to trim down in *40-Year-Old Virgin* which was Steve Carell watching a porno and fast-forwarding past the sex to get to the parts where they talk. You didn't really see anything. You just saw people moving very quickly and maybe boobs shaking really fast, but no penetration or anything. But the test audiences were really freaked out. I thought people would really laugh at super-sped-up sex.

CERA: They do that in *Clockwork Orange* where they have that sequence where everybody's having sex really fast.

APATOW: I didn't have that Kubrickian touch.

ROGEN: We didn't have Beethoven's Fifth.

Q. *Is there always a struggle to find the appropriate line on things like that?*

APATOW: The audience tells you very quickly where the line is.

ROGEN: But, like, the period-blood scene [in *Superbad*], we didn't have any options. We did paint ourselves into a corner, just hoping people would go with it. And people went with it for the most part, thank God, or we'd be reshooting right now.

HILL: I remember that night, too, because Michael and I weren't allowed to go to the first test screening in case something went horribly wrong.

APATOW: Just in case they hated you and you'd never get off the couch. Here's how that call goes: "Jonah wants to go to the first screening." "No! Because if they hate him, he'll never recover!"

HILL: But I remember the second everyone called me and e-mailed me at the same time. Judd sent me a few e-mails, one being like, "It's crazy, it's awesome, everyone loved it." And a second later he sent another one: "Even period-blood killed," with five exclamation points.

ROGEN: I think that's the most nervous I've ever been in my life, at that first screening when the period-blood scene started. We would have had to reshoot something. I was horrified, absolutely horrified.

APATOW: It's so gross we can't even talk about it in *EW*. This whole section won't be in there.

Q. *Judd, I know you've been a big believer in showing your movies to test audiences and if they don't laugh at something, you throw it out. Some people might wonder if you risk squeezing the idiosyncrasies out that way.*

APATOW: Well, usually as you're about to lock a movie, you throw in 15 jokes that didn't work just for yourself. "We're about to lock forever—put back in that thing everybody hates."

ROGEN: But if there's something we love, we'll keep it generally. I mean, even the "Age of Aquarius" thing in *Virgin*—people didn't like it for the most part.

APATOW: That's not true. People liked it. Well, here's the thing with all testing: The favorite thing is always also the least favorite. Out of 400 people, 100 people will say something is their favorite thing and then like 35 or 40 will say it's their least favorite. On dirty things, on clean things, there's always that split. But that hasn't become an issue that we disagree with the audience. In fact, when those audiences walk out of these tests now, they look exactly like the cast. You couldn't tell. It's like if the band Wilco had 400 members.

ROGEN: Exactly. We're like the Polyphonic Spree.

HILL: Do you think that's it? Are people finally wanting to see people that they recognize from their lives?

APATOW: Those people always existed. There's more people now. But it's not like suddenly *Freaks and Geeks* sold 10 million DVDs in the last six months.

Q. *But I assume it's easier for you now to sell people on your theory that you don't need recognizable faces in comedy—you just need people who are funny.*

APATOW: I've always had a simple theory, which is that movies that are genuinely funny never bomb. Then people say, "What about *Office Space*?" And I say, "It was a huge hit on DVD."

Q. *So TV is different?*

APATOW: TV is different because you can be in the wrong time slot and just never get seen.

commentaries... seriously!

Superbad

Q. *Was that what happened with* Arrested Development?

APATOW: But that kept going on for three years.
CERA: I was surprised it kept getting picked up.

Q. *It survived just solely on glowing reviews.*

CERA: Yeah, critics. And we won Emmys the first year. But nobody ever was watching and it went three years.
APATOW: But in movies, if something is very funny and people laugh, it never is a money-loser for somebody. So I always say, I don't think people care who's in a movie at all. It may be a marketing challenge. *Superbad* is a bit of a marketing challenge.
HILL: What about, like, *Ace Ventura*? I remember when that came out, I knew who Jim Carrey was from *In Living Color*, but, like, my parents didn't know who he was. No one knew who he was.
ROGEN: I remember I was so psyched for the new "James Carrey" movie. *[Laughs]* People like to be the first guy to discover somebody.
HILL: And then they hate us when we become successful.
ROGEN: I remember when *Ali G* came on, nothing made me happier than to tell someone who hadn't heard about it to watch it. It's the same with movies. You want to be the guy to tell your friends. Like *Foot Fist Way*—I tell everyone about that, because then people think you're funnier. It reflects well upon you.
HILL: It's like wearing a shirt of a band. People associate you with the coolness of the band.
APATOW: I remember someone once sent me the pilot of *South Park*. And someone called me to give some advice about how you hire a staff, so I talked to Matt Stone and I said, "I just want to be the first one to say this to you. This is going to be the biggest thing ever. I just want to say this so it's official. Everybody's jumping on the train—I want to jump on first. This is going to be crazy, cover of *Rolling Stone*. Your life is completely destroyed from this point." I had nothing to do with any aspect of the show, but my cool factor in my own mind went up.
ROGEN: Maybe people who want to be viewed as really smart and intellectual tell people to go see *Babel*, but people who want to be funny will tell everyone to go see *Office Space*. I think that's just how it is. It reflects upon you in a way.

Q. *You don't get more satisfaction getting a laugh from—*

APATOW: From a bitter comedian?

Q. *Yeah, the comedy experts—getting a laugh from them doesn't mean more to you?*

APATOW: No, no, I turned on them a long time ago.
ROGEN: There are jokes that our snobby movie friends can over-intellectualize laughing at, but we didn't write it for them. We write it for regular people. We don't make these movies for people who are really into movies necessarily.
HILL: I make everything I do for Michael. If I see that little smile, it makes my whole day worthwhile.
CERA: I make my playlist on my iPod based on what Jonah would like—and he's never even going to listen to it.

Superbad

Q. *A lot of comedy these days—Borat, Curb Your Enthusiasm, your movies—comes out of awkwardness and discomfort. Is it tough to find the line sometimes between funny-awkward and just plain painful?*

ROGEN: When it makes me so uncomfortable I want to turn it off, that's when I know I'm watching something awesome. Like, I remember the first time I saw the British *Office*, I was like, Oh, my God. I literally couldn't watch it all at once, because it made me so uncomfortable. That's when I realized, like, F---, these guys are good. Especially when you know it's fake.

APATOW: When I was a kid, I used to watch *The Honeymooners* and as soon as they got to the moment where everything was going to collapse, I'd shut it off and didn't come back. I watched the first 12 minutes of every *Honeymooners*. Now I do almost nothing but cringe-factor comedy, but I just couldn't handle it at all. My favorite show now is *Extras*. It makes me laugh so hard. But that's another one where I have to pause.

HILL: I feel like in life sometimes I create those situations because I find them funny. Like I'm consciously trying to create an uncomfortable situation because I find that funny.

ROGEN: Michael does that.

HILL: You thrive on that, yeah.

CERA: I'll go to a party sometimes that I can't stand being at, and I'll just sit there listening to people. Just people I don't want to be around.

Q. *Do you all have a really high tolerance for awkwardness?*

APATOW: In life? My whole life is an awkward moment. Every single day I'm awkward so much of the day.

ROGEN: It's funny hanging out with [*Superbad* cowriter] Evan [Goldberg] a lot, because he creates a lot of awkwardness but he is never uncomfortable.

CERA: I find that elderly people are like that. Elderly people have no sense of awkward situations. I can't wait to be like that.

ROGEN: I'm always so awkward and always reading into situations and thinking about how other people are interpreting something that they're probably not even thinking about. Then I just see Evan in his underwear in the middle of the street, like, "So what are we doing, dudes?"

Q. *A lot of critics and commentators—the David Denbys and Maureen Dowds of the world—have tagged your brand of comedy as, essentially, immature guy humor about immature guys.*

ROGEN: Made for, by, and about immature guys.

APATOW: Whenever I read any of that stuff, I always think, There's literally no history of mature-guy humor. Go watch *Modern Times*: Charlie Chaplin has two wrenches and he's chasing after a woman with nuts on her nipples! I mean, there is no mature comedy. Even those old Cary Grant movies, I think they're all immature and weird.

ROGEN: Is Preston Sturges mature?

HILL: Is *Sideways* a mature comedy?

APATOW: I reject the entire notion of maturity. Nothing is funny that is mature. Isn't it all just doing things wrong and screwing up and learning lessons?

commentaries... seriously!

ROGEN: *Network* is a good mature comedy.
APATOW: No, it's immature, because it's an old man screwing a young woman. He can't grow up! He has to cheat on his wonderful wife with Faye Dunaway.

Q. *The process on these movies seems very different from a show like* Arrested Development, *where actors stuck closely to the words.*

CERA: Well, [*Arrested Development* had] very meticulously written jokes, but it wasn't very strict. You could say whatever you want after you did the first take.
ROGEN: Often, time just dictates that. You just don't have a whole day to shoot one scene. That's what's nice about a movie.
APATOW: We have way too much time. *Larry Sanders*, they shot the show in two days, 17 pages a day. Shoot a scene in an hour, shoot another scene in an hour. There wasn't much time to play around.

Q. *You guys do a huge amount of improvising in these movies. Is that hard for some actors to get used to?*

APATOW: Most people who are funny can improvise if they relax and allow themselves to think they can. The ratio of success can be very low and it can still be very helpful to the movie. Katherine Heigl never thought she could improvise and she was fantastic at it. She left the audition thinking she didn't get it, and we were like, "Oh my God, that was awesome." So it's hard to tell.
ROGEN: I've never met anyone that we've worked with who just can't do it. Especially the way we work. All our scenes are based in reality and conversational. I always said to Katherine Heigl, "It's not like I'll be like, 'So where should we go for dinner?' And you'll just be like, 'Uh, uh. . . I don't know!'"
APATOW: "There's no dinner in the script!" [*Laughs*]
ROGEN: If you can listen to the question, you can probably do it.

Q. *But to come up with something funny and also move the scene where it needs to go—*

APATOW: Well, we always talk about it before it happens and we'll throw people lines or ideas or areas. People aren't really just hanging out there on the line.
HILL: I think a lot of it is being so scared not to do it, you just do it. If someone put you in that position and there's cameras around and you didn't do it, you'd feel so s----y.
APATOW: My 9-year-old daughter did it on the first day. That's what I'm going to say on the rest of my movies if an actor can't improvise: "My f---ing 3-year-old did it! She could improvise with a s--- in her pants!"
HILL: What is being really funny if you can't improvise and create your own kind of thing?
APATOW: There are people who are just interpreters. David Mamet doesn't want you to improvise.
ROGEN: And that's why he's so funny. [*Laughs*]

Q. *Not every comedy director would be so open to improvising. I don't know that Woody Allen loves a lot of ad-libbing on his set.*

APATOW: He will let you change a line—at least that's what they say. I don't know if anyone has the courage to do it, but I think the invitation is there.

ROGEN: I would. It would be so funny if I worked on a Woody Allen movie and I didn't say one thing he wrote. "Thanks for the suggestions."

APATOW: You're three months away from being in a Woody Allen movie, by the way.

HILL: As you said that, I was thinking, "*Jew in New York*, starring Seth Rogen." I guarantee Seth will be in a Woody Allen movie. But you'll be in one of the serious crime-thriller Woody Allen movies. You're going to kill Scarlett Johansson.

ROGEN: *Match Point 2: The Rogening.*

Q. *Michael, was it intimidating for you to come in and have to work that way, with so much improv?*

CERA: Definitely. But we did rehearsals for a month beforehand where we'd hang out at Seth's house and we did a bunch of table reads. I felt like I knew it really well, and we were so comfortable around each other.

ROGEN: We set a precedent pretty early. One of the first things we did when they were all cast was we had them over to my apartment and we went through the script line by line and just said, "How would you say this line? What would you say there?" We made it clear, "We don't give a s---. Say whatever the hell you want." Why hire Michael Cera if you're not going to let him do that s---?

APATOW: You can't really fight over the specific syntax and language of a d--- joke. You can't be that proud of it.

Q. *Obviously, the advantage of having people improvise is that it gives you things you can't come up with in advance. But at the same time, doesn't it make it harder to cut the film together at the end?*

APATOW: That's why I wanted Greg to direct *Superbad*. He's just a fantastic writer, and I knew in the final polish stages of the script, he would make sure the emotional aspects of the movie worked really well and he would find that balance. That's why he so outclasses us in his abilities. He took something that could have been very base and awful and made it. . . I mean, it's funny and filthy but it's also a beautiful movie about friendship and people cry at the end of the movie when these guys have to part. It gets me every time.

HILL: What always pisses me off is when you'll hear, like, five dudes laughing at the ending. It makes them too uncomfortable, so they go "huh-huh."

commentaries... seriously!

CERA: It's too real.
APATOW: "Feelings! Emotions! Must shut them down! Punch someone!" Well, the movie always was about guys who are afraid of intimacy covering it up with this incredible bravado and talking about what they're going to do to women, and it's all bulls---.
ROGEN: The joke to me and Evan was always, like, in the first five minutes of the movie they could have walked up to these women and asked them on dates and the movie would have ended right there. The whole movie takes place as an excuse for them not to actually talk to these girls.
APATOW: Because there is nothing scarier than that. I've never walked up to a girl in a bar once in my entire life. I've never had the courage to see someone and talk to them. So I always relate to that story.

Q. *Are there clichés or setups in studio comedies that you feel are just so played out, you can't stand them anymore?*

ROGEN: I like it all. If *Knocked Up* taught us anything, it's that you can take an idea that's very sitcomy and clichéd and if you approach it from an original standpoint it won't be.

Q. *I have to say, the logline on* Superbad: *two geeky guys trying to buy beer—*

HILL: It sounds like the worst movie ever.
ROGEN: It doesn't just sound like the worst movie. It sounds like a million other movies.
HILL: Seth and I were talking about making a grindhouse double-feature: *Boner Party* and *Boobie School*. *[Laughs]*

Q. *Judd, you've developed this sort of repertory company of actors and cowriters who are significantly younger than you. There's a 20-year age difference between you and Michael here.*

APATOW: Jesus Christ, this just took a very dark turn. You son of a bitch. And thus began the beginning of my creative paralysis. *[Laughs]* It's true, though, I could be Michael Cera's dad. I could be everyone's dad here if I started having sex at 14.

Q. *From the outside, it seems unusual that you guys manage to work so well together and have such similar sensibilities.*

ROGEN: It's funny, when I met Judd and learned about all the stuff he did, I realized that's the stuff that directly influenced me. I mean, like, Adam Sandler's comedy albums were gold to me. Those were the first things that made me think, S---, there are things you can do with comedy I never thought you could. And Judd helped out with those.
APATOW: Very little.
ROGEN: And *The Ben Stiller Show* and *Larry Sanders*. All those things were huge.
HILL: That's how I found out who Judd was. I kind of compiled a bunch of s--- that I liked and his name was in the group of that the most.
ROGEN: You did a Bible-code-type thing.
HILL: I did a *Beautiful Mind*. But that's how I figured it out, because I kept seeing his name on s--- I thought was cool. *[To Apatow]* How does that make you feel, dude?
ROGEN: You're responsible for this filth.
APATOW: I feel so old right now. My wife was

45

watching the trailer for *Superbad* and it says, "From the guy who brought you *40-Year-Old Virgin* and *Knocked Up*," and she just turned to me and went, "Great, now you've become that guy." *[Laughs]*

Q. *Judd, it must surprise you to find a guy like Michael, whose sense of comedy is so highly developed at age 19.*

APATOW: I am surprised because I was so unfunny at that age. I mean, I was really not funny at all at 16, 17, 18, 19. I look back at old standup tapes and notebooks and it was really godawful and embarrassing. So yeah, to see guys who really know what they're doing and are sophisticated, it makes me ashamed of everything I did in those years. I think back to being around all those comics I admired, having them see my act and how bad it was—that's brutal. I remember being booed off the stage at UC Santa Barbara. I was opening up for Marc "Skippy" Price from *Family Ties*. I was terrible. I had a lot of jokes about condoms: "My grandfather gave me a condom. It was made out of wicker." That was about the level of the act. It wasn't really at the *Arrested Development* level.

HILL: That's what's always so f---ing embarrassing to me, is that Seth and Michael have only done awesome s---. And when you saw Aint-It-Cool.com stuff before *Superbad*, the review would start out, "Trust me, Jonah Hill is funny. Please believe us. Seriously, I know, I think he sucks, too, but then I saw this movie." I'd had to do s--- I wasn't super-psyched about. But all my friends have the most flawless careers of all time.

APATOW: Hey, George Clooney was in *The Facts of Life*. I always said to Seth from the beginning, "Don't do anything crappy. Keep the résumé looking good so when you get your opportunity people aren't burned out on you."

ROGEN: When I was younger, I always wondered, Why does Judd hang out with me? Doesn't he feel weird?

APATOW: Is he some kind of a pedophile?

ROGEN: But honestly, since I've met Michael, I'm like seven years older than you and it literally doesn't occur to me for a second that I'm older than you. And I'm glad because it finally gives me some insight into what it was like when people hung out with me and I was so much younger than them.

Q. *Michael, does that mean you're sitting around feeling self-conscious about how much older these guys are than you?*

HILL: Well, we molest Michael. It's a different vibe.

ROGEN: We were saying, if Michael's career doesn't go well, he could be the kid on *To Catch a Predator*.

CERA: *[In high, boyish voice]* "Did you bring the vodka? I'm going to get changed. I just got out the shower. I'm drying my hair. Sit down, there's some cookies over there."

Q. *Where do you guys go for comedy? Jonah and Michael, I know you two are big Zach Galifianakis fans.*

ROGEN: He's hilarious. I love *Extras*. *The Office*.

CERA: There's a [British] show called *Garth Marenghi's Dark Place*. That's the most brilliant show.

HILL: I love Edgar Wright's movies. *The Mighty*

commentaries... seriously!

Boosh on the BBC is really funny.

Q. *So with the winning streak you've been on, where do you go from here? Do you think it can continue or do you have a sense of doom?*

APATOW: I'm always trying to think of people who've had careers that have lasted more than four months. That's how I'm choosing to get through this. Like, okay, these people have made some decent movies over a 10- to 25-year period. It wasn't just a little summer. Look at Larry Gelbart. Look at Carl Reiner. Look at Mel Brooks. He's having hits at 80. He's doing *Young Frankenstein* on Broadway. It's possible next year won't suck. *[Laughs]*

ROGEN: I've had some good luck, so I'm always thinking something terrible is going to happen. But then I'm like, Look at George Clooney. He's done way more movies than us—and he's really handsome. Nothing terrible's happened to him. It just keeps getting better and better.

APATOW: The postscript to this is: "Judd nibbled some dog food made in China and dropped dead on the spot."

ROGEN: "Oddly, a meteor hit the table, killing Michael, Seth, Judd, and Jonah. Josh and his tape recorder were completely unscathed."

HILL: I'll bet you $1,000 that's how this interview ends. ■

47

Mr. Vagtastic's Guide to Buying Porn

by Matt "Mr. Vagtastic" Bass

So you wanna buy some porn, eh? This is a difficult decision, one which will make or break a boner. Some people are disgusted by the mere presence of penetration, others are totally turned off by the facial. If you fall into these categories, I'd hate for you to rent *Facial Paint #6* or *Anal Canyons #4*. So please, to avoid this issue, take the time and thoroughly read the Vagtastic criteria to purchasing porn.

KNOW YOUR FETISH
Don't be scared off by the term *fetish*—it's just a fancy, perverted word for *genre*. If you want to feel like you're part of the action, go for the POV. If you dig the passionate union of different ethnicities, check out Interracial. Tired of external cum shots and want to see a guy finish the old-fashioned way, pick up some Creampie action. Don't be that sucker who wants to watch hot threesome action and accidentally picks out Toys and Trannies.

KNOW YOUR CONTRACT GIRLS
People argue that gonzo is the way to go, because

Mr. Vagtastic's Guide to Buying Porn

it's real girls in real situations, but when you dream of buying a car, what do you picture, a Hyundai or a Porsche? Let your wildest fantasies indulge themselves. Don't pick up *Big Dick in Little China*; rather, select from the top production studios. Know the girls that turn you on and read the box covers carefully.

ALWAYS JUDGE A MOVIE BY ITS COVER
Box covers don't lie. They have the girls on the front to entice you and pictures of the scenes you'll be viewing on the back. So if you want to spank it to some hot girl-on-girl action, check the back to make sure the movie contains such a scene.

WITHIN ARMS' REACH
You never know when Lil' Peter Pan wants to fly to Neverland, so you need to make sure visual stimulation is always at arms' reach. Those lonely nights in hotel rooms call for a romantic party of one. If you can access fuzzy porn, give it a go. It's free tits and it teaches your eyes to focus on even the smallest fragment of vagina. If you're gonna pay the piper and order the pay per view, make sure the bill doesn't go to Mr. Bossman. What about those long overseas flights? Fourteen hours sandwiched between a showering salesman and the rep for some overpriced perfume may trigger some movement downstairs. For this I recommend the newest technology.

An MP3 player that stores video or even a new fancy phone that holds megapixels of fellatio. At a time like this I recommend keeping pictures of old girlfriends. Nothing says boner like an ex-lover holding your boner. But please do me a favor—don't let those pictures get out or you'll ruin it for everyone.

THE MORAL
In conclusion, follow these simple steps and I guarantee you'll be tooting your horn to the perfect porn. People may question your activities, but the art of porn selection is a fine science. Take your time and never be embarrassed or ashamed. Remember, there is a reason why porn is a multibillion-dollar-a-year industry. If any one bothers you, just tell them your friendly neighborhood Vagtastic Voyager sent you. ■

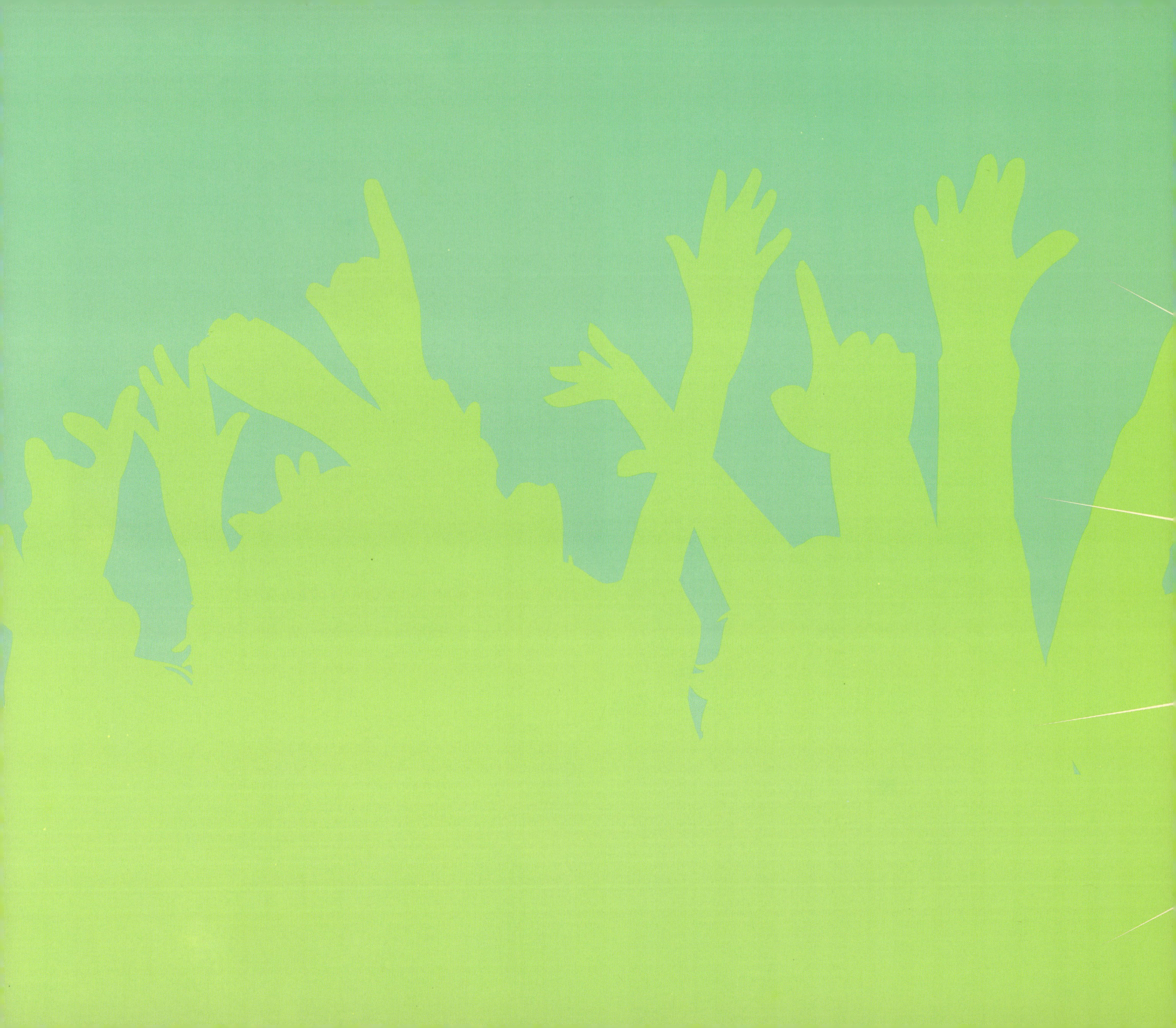

The Penis Gallery

Superbad

McLovin, Seth and Evan on the Bus

52

Contemplating My Penises

My name is David Goldberg and I created the penis drawings for the movie *Superbad*. When I first got a call from my younger brother Evan (*Superbad*'s co-writer/producer) saying he had a job for me on his upcoming film *Superbad*, I was confused as to what he might need from me. When I found out what he wanted was for me to draw a multitude of penises for him I was, admittedly, still quite confused. However, I assumed he and his partner Seth knew what they were doing, so, to the shock of many of my friends, draw penises is exactly what I did.

It was the beginning of a weird and wonderful time in my life; however, not everyone knew how to respond to my newfound hobby. Sure, they look cool on the silver screen in a feature presentation, but when your small apartment is littered with piles of crumpled-up penis drawings that just weren't good enough to make the final cut, or when you quickly jot down an outline of a penis drawing in the middle of a conversation during dinner so you don't forget it. . . people tend to look at you strangely. Even if the people in question already know that the various illustrations are going to be used for a movie, you still get the feeling that most people think you're a little bit weird.

I had to wait until *Superbad* was released in theaters for my vindication. Then the strange things weren't the weird looks I'd get, but the far more bizarre compliments I'd receive from friends and strangers on my penises (which, in turn, got some strange looks from anyone within earshot who didn't know what we were talking about). Or even stranger still, the people who utterly refused to believe that I hadn't always drawn penises and that I was simply doing it because that's what I'd been asked to do.

Yet for all the weirdness, there was a great deal of gratification involved in creating these drawings for *Superbad*. There's a Zen-like euphoria that goes hand in hand with such projects and you get such a feeling of fulfillment that I've yet to find its equal. Knowing that not only are you drawing penises, but that you're making a difference in this world and bringing joy into people's lives is a wonderful, beautiful thing. It may be that I'm being overly sentimental now that it's all over. . . or it may just be that those were the best days of my life.

— David Goldberg

Gunslinger Penis

Superbad

Platoon Penis

The Greek Pantheon Penises

54

The Penis Gallery

Angel Penis Flying Over Hell

Pirate Penis

55

Superbad

Aquarium Fish

56

The Penis Gallery

Tiananmen Square Penis

Torture Chamber Penises

Iwo Jima Penis

Roman Battle Penis

Superbad

Smoking Mushroom Penis

Fish Hook Penis

Evolution Penis

The Penis Gallery

Titanic Penis

59

SUPERBAD

SUPERBAD

The complete screenplay
by Seth Rogen & Evan Goldberg

SUPERBAD

OPENING CREDITS OVER SUPER-FUNKY BLAXPLOITATION-STYLE MUSIC, which builds to an exciting crescendo that fills us with the expectation of a thrilling, action-packed opening sequence.

Instead we get:

INT. SETH'S CAR – MORNING

Seth, seventeen and clearly a terrible driver, cruises along, enjoying the funk tune. The song starts to skip. He angrily punches the CD player with his fist. He looks up to see he is driving right towards some garbage cans. He swerves erratically and narrowly avoids them.

He pulls out his cell and dials.

>SETH
>Yo.

INTERCUT WITH:

INT. EVAN'S HOUSE – KITCHEN – CONTINUOUS

Evan, seventeen, a little too tall and slim, is finishing off a bowl of cereal. He is on his cell phone.

>EVAN
>What's up?

>SETH
>I was doing research last night, for next year, and I think I know which web-page I'm gonna subscribe to next year. The Vag-tastic Voyage.

>EVAN
>Which one's Vag-tastic Voyage?

>SETH
>The one where they pick up random girls on the street and take them in a van and bang 'em. Thirteen bucks a month. And you get access to all these other sites, like, Latina, one's Asian, fetishes for, like, feet and pee and shit like that, all for the price of Vag-tastic Voyage.

>EVAN
>You are absolutely disgusting. You're like an animal.

>SETH
>Don't make me seem weird because I like porn. You're weird 'cause you don't like porn. I'm normal as shit.

>EVAN
>Peeing on people. That's normal?

>SETH
>I'm not saying I'm gonna look at it, I'm saying it comes with it. Who knows what I'll be into one day.

>EVAN
>And I hate that amateur stuff. If I'm paying money, I want some production value; smooth editing, a good score, not some girls being coaxed into going on a vag-tastic voyage.

>SETH
>I'm sorry that the Coen Brother's didn't direct the porno I watch.

>EVAN
>And plus, your parents are gonna look at the bill, smart-guy.

>SETH
>Maybe I should just pick the one that's name will look the least dirty.

Seth pulls up in front of a house.

EXT. EVAN'S HOUSE – CONTINUOUS

Evan walks out his front door. WE REVEAL he is walking towards Seth's car.

>EVAN
>Something like "Perfect 10" could be any number of things.

>SETH
>Yeah, but they don't actually show dick going in, which is a huge concern.

They both hang up and Evan gets in the car. Seth is about to pull away, when EVAN'S MOTHER comes out the front door.

>EVAN'S MOM
>Thanks for taking him, Seth.

Evan reaches to the stereo. Seth slaps his hand.

SETH
Don't touch that!

EVAN'S MOM
You two are so funny. I can't imagine what you'll do without each other next year. Evan told me you didn't get into Dartmouth.

SETH
Yeah, you know. I really like to talk about that. I got in some other places. Good places. I think we'll be fine.

EVAN'S MOM
Are you going to miss each other?

EVAN
Miss each other? No!

SETH
That's disgusting.

MOM
Bye, boys.

Seth and Evan drive off.

SETH
I am truly, truly jealous that you got to suck on those tits when you were a baby.

EVAN
Well, at least you got to suck your Dad's dick.

SETH
I just kissed the tip a little – it's a nice dick.

EXT. CLARK SECONDARY – SOON AFTER

They drive up to Clark Secondary. There is a giant sign that reads "Seniors – Two Glorious Weeks Until Graduation". Seth turns into the STAFF parking lot.

INT/EXT. SPEEDY MART – MOMENTS LATER

Seth and Evan walk past a group of smokers, towards the 7-11.

EVAN
You're being an idiot, man. You really shouldn't park there.

SETH
Fuck it. I'm a senior about to graduate. They should be suckin' my balls. It's the least they can do for stealing three years of my life.

They walk past DIMITRI (18, big Native American guy) as they enter the store. Dimitri aggressively bumps his shoulder into Seth.

EVAN
What the hell's wrong with Dimitri?

SETH
Oh, yeah dude, I forgot to tell you. I knocked the shit out of him in capture the flag last week.

EVAN
Good! I hate that guy.

They go to the magazine rack and stare at a magazine cover.

EVAN (CONT'D)
Look at those nipples.

SETH
They're like baby toes.

EVAN
It's not fair they can just flaunt that stuff. I have to hide every erection I get.

SETH
I flip it up into my waistband. Hides it, and feels awesome. I've almost blown a load into my belly button from it.

EVAN
Just imagine if girls weren't weirded out by our boners and they actually wanted to see 'em and stuff.

SETH
It's been, like, two years since I've seen an actual human female nipple. Besides my mom's. I saw it last month, and it was sick.

Superbad

                    EVAN
Holy shit. Shauna was two years ago? I guess
so. She was insanely hot, though.

                    SETH
Exactly. Too hot. That's what sucks.

                    EVAN
How can that possibly suck? I'd be psyched if
I'd gotten with a girl that hot. You got, like, two
dozen handjobs!

                    SETH
And three quarters of a blowjob, but whose
counting? It was the peak of my ass-gettin'
career, and it happened way, way, way too early.

                    EVAN
You're like Orson Welles.

                    SETH
Exactly! If I'd built up to it, I'd probably at least
be having steady sex with a normal girl at this
point. I honestly now see why Orson Welles ate
his fat ass to death.

                    EVAN
You'll have sex in college. Everyone does.

                    SETH
But the key is to be good at sex by the time
you're in college. You don't want girls to think
you suck dick at fucking pussy.

                    EVAN
I still think you've got a chance with Jules. She
got hot over last summer, and clearly hasn't
realized it, 'cause she still flirts with you.

                    SETH
Are you joking, man? Look at who she's dated!
Dan Remick, who's had a six pack since like,
kindergarten. Jason Stone, who looks like
fuckin' Zack Morris, and Matt Muir! Matt Muir!!
He's like the sweetest guy ever. Have you seen
him smile? Why would she end her high school
career with me?

                    EVAN
Becca dated Eric Rosecrantz for two years.

                    SETH
Yeah, and he was a complete fucking loser.
You're actually a step up from that dick-load.
That's why you've gotta stop being a pussy and
do her! You could nail the shit out of her for,
like, two months before you leave. And she looks
like a good fucker.

                    EVAN
Hey! I'm sick of you talking about her like that,
man!

Evan starts to walk out. Seth follows.

                    SETH
What, you can talk about her all day every
single day, but I can't say one thing?

                    EVAN
I don't constantly insult her.

                    SETH
You're misunderstanding me. I'm not trying
to insult her. I just said she looks like a good
fucker. Like she can take a dick. That's a good
thing. Some women pride themselves on their
dick-taking abilities.

                    EVAN
"Dick-taking abilities?" You don't actually think
that's a good thing to say, do you?

                    SETH
What's fucked up is, I do. I mean, I'd be psyched
if people talked about my dick-giving ability.
Right?

EXT. SPEEDY MART – CONTINUOUS

Seth and Evan come out the front doors. JESSE, one of the rough-looking
smokers, calls out.

                    JESSE
Yo. Seth.

SETH
What, Jesse?

JESSE
Did you hear I'm having the big grad party?

Evan, a little scared, keeps his distance.

SETH
No.

JESSE
Yeah.

Jesse spits on Seth's shirt.

JESSE (CONT'D)
And you're not coming. Tell your fucking faggot friend he can't come either.

Seth wipes the spit off. He looks at Jesse and seems as though he's about to say something, but is interrupted when Jesse starts hocking up more spit. Seth runs away as Jesse and his friends laugh. He catches up to Evan and they head back to school.

EVAN
Wow. You really bitched out on that one.

SETH
I bitched out? You bitched out! You were across the street before I even realized what was going on.
(beat)
That guy's such a douche bag.

EXT. CLARK SECONDARY OVAL RUNNING TRACK – DAY

Bird's eye view of a p.e. class

There are 30 guys standing behind the starting line of the school's track. We hear a TEACHER yell "Go!" and the boys start running.

We FOLLOW them from above. All the boys keep pretty much the same pace except for one runner who slowly lags behind. The group gets so far ahead of the him that he is alone in the frame. He stops.

Close up of THE RUNNER:

Kneeling on the track breathing heavily. It's Seth.

SETH
(panting)
This. . . is. . . bullshit.

A moment later a KID with prosthetic leg jogs by.

KID
(as he passes Seth)
Poo-say.

INT. CLARK SECONDARY CLASSROOM – DAY

Evan is sitting in math class staring at Becca's breasts. She's a very small girl. He looks up from her breasts to her face: she is staring right at him. He immediately looks to the front of the class, embarrassed.

The bell rings and everyone leaves. Becca walks up to Evan as they enter the hallway. He's really nervous. She offers him a pen.

BECCA
Hey Evan, thanks for the pen.

EVAN
Oh, don't worry, no worries. Just keep it. Then you'll just have it, and you won't have to borrow another pen.

BECCA
Thanks. . . uh. . . I was going to ask you, did you hear about Jesse's grad party? That should be fun, huh?

EVAN
Yeah, it's a maybe. But, you know, I gotta, I got my. . . there's so much other fun shit that is going to be going on that night. . . so, you know. . .

BECCA
Fun shit? But I never see you at any parties or anything.

EVAN
Because of all the other fun shit I'm off doing.

BECCA
(playful)
Okay. So why weren't you at Dimitri's party on Saturday? You must have heard about it. Him

Screenplay

and Dan Vertlieb stole a keg from Goodshopper. It was crazy.

                    EVAN
        I uh. . . didn't want to go, because, well, I did
        other stuff. Saturday. . .
            (nervous, he desperately thinks)
        Oh yeah! Saturday night was awesome! Off the
        hook.

SPLIT SCREEN: The real version of Evan's story is shown through a montage of quick flashbacks.

                    EVAN (CONT'D)
        First my parents went out to a double feature,
        so a bunch of people came over. . .

INT. EVAN'S HOUSE – NIGHT

Seth is there. Evan and him are surfing the Bang Bus web site. FOGELL arrives with a bottle of Sambuca. Fogell is one of those seniors who looks like he's thirteen years old.

                    EVAN
        . . . and we had a couple drinks in my
        basement, just mellowing, ya know? The chill-
        zone. . .

An empty bottle of Sambuca in front of them and empty beer cans at their feet, the three boys each shotgun a beer.

                    EVAN (CONT'D) (V.O)
        . . . and Seth's parents were having this cocktail
        party, and we went over there to, like, mingle. . .

EXT SETH'S BACKYARD – NIGHT

Seth's parents are having an exclusively adult backyard summer cook-out. The boys stumble in, drunk as hell.

                    EVAN
        . . . and there were actually some really inter-
        esting and, like, entertaining people there. . .

The boys laugh hysterically as they each shake Tabasco sauce onto their tongues. They writhe around in agony as several adults look at them like they are morons.

                    EVAN (CONT'D) (V.O.)
        . . . and, uh, then we saw some, uh, live music.
        Which is a nice activity. . .

EXT. SETH'S BACKYARD – LATER ON

The adults have lost interest in the boys, who now violently wrestle on the nearby lawn. Evan gives Fogell a bloody nose, but they all can't help but laugh.

                    EVAN
        . . . then we went to a club downtown. . .

EXT. STRIP CLUB – NIGHT

The bouncer of a dirty strip club rejects them.

                    EVAN
        . . . and then we pretty much called it a night
        and went home. . .

EXT. SIDEWALK – NIGHT

Seth urges Evan and Fogell to hurry up. He grabs Evan's collar and tugs him forward, causing Evan to puke all over Seth. Evan and Fogell laugh hysterically as Seth explodes in rage.

INT. CLARK SECONDARY HALLWAY – DAY

We return to Evan talking to Becca in the halls.

                    EVAN
        . . . you would've loved it.

                    BECCA
        That sounds so fun. I would love to go do
        something like that.

                    EVAN
        Yeah. . . well, you know, me and Seth are always
        cooking up. . . uh. . . fun little. . . events.

Becca is disappointed in his response.

                    BECCA
        Yeah. I bet you guys are really going to go
        crazy next year.

                    EVAN
        Nah. We were going to but, uh, we got into
        different schools.

BECCA
Oh. That sucks.

EVAN
Whatever. It's not that bad. It'll be fine. Don't worry about it. I'm not.

INT. FOODS AND NUTRITION ROOM – NEXT PERIOD

Students file into the home economics room. The blackboard reads, TODAY: TIRAMISU. The ingredients are listed below.

Seth is talking to the cooking teacher.

SETH
Mrs. Hayworth, I joined this class because I thought I'd be cooking with a partner. She's never here. I don't get twice the marks for doing all the work.

MRS. HAYWORTH
I didn't invent odd numbers, Seth.

SETH
Look at Evan.

Evan is playfully throwing flour at a tiny Japanese boy. They both laugh hard.

SETH (CONT'D)
While I'm over in my unit, isolated and alone, eating my terrible-tasting food, I gotta look over at that.

The Japanese boy ties Evan's apron. Evan then turns around and ties the boy's apron. They both look happy.

SETH (CONT'D)
I wash and dry. And that is B.S. I'm like a single mother.

MRS. HAYWORTH
Today Jules' partner isn't here either. Pair up with her. Station four.

The teacher walks away. Seth looks over to station four, nervous as hell.

ANGLE ON: Jules, well-dressed and "popular" looking. She stands alone at station four, laying out utensils.

Seth musters his courage and walks towards Jules. He stops, unsure of what to say.

SETH
Hey Jules, your partner didn't come today?

JULES
That's kind of a personal question.

SETH
What?

JULES
Nothing. It was my attempt at humour.

SETH
Oh! Like cumming!
(jerk off hand gesture)
Cumming coming. Ha. Yeah. My partner never comes. I don't think she's ever come. Except the class where we made banana splits.

JULES
Wow. Too far.

SETH
Yeah. Way. I do that.

JULES
Don't worry. I'm used to it. My older brother always says, like, the nastiest shit. He called me Hymen until I was twelve.

SETH
That's sick! That's not even clever.

JULES
I know! I would have gone for something like "Family Jules".

Seth laughs, completely smitten.

SETH
Ha! That's a fucking awesome joke.

MUSIC UP: IT MUST HAVE BEEN LOVE by ROXETTE.

Screenplay

Superbad

A series of images where we see that Seth is hitting on Jules.

— As they lay out the cooking utensils, Seth uses any opportunity he can to brush up against Jules.

— Jules gets some sugar in her hair and Seth awkwardly helps her get it out.

— Evan tries to get Seth's attention so he can show him that he's painted flour on Miroki's face to make him look like a kitty-cat. Seth motions for Evan to get lost so he can focus on Jules.

— They chat as they lick the excess batter off the utensils. Jules says something hilarious that makes Seth laugh hard.

— Jules washes some utensils as Seth checks out her ass.

INT. FOODS AND NUTRITION ROOM – LATER

Jules watches as Seth awkwardly removes the tiramisu from the oven and places it on the table.

> JULES
> What are you doing tonight?

> SETH
> I don't know, probably nothing. Why?

> JULES
> My parents are out of town and I'm thinking of having a party. I don't know how big it'll be, but you should come anyways.

> SETH
> Yeah. Sure. That sounds fun. I love parties.

> JULES
> Really? I don't usually see you at them.

> SETH
> Oh, uh. It's more of, like, a love-hate thing. Right now I love them, though.

ANGLE ON: Evan.

Evan is standing by the sink scrubbing a tray. Behind him, at the table, is the small Japanese boy eating the tiramisu.

> EVAN
> That's good shit. Huh, Miroki?

Seth walks up to Evan.

> SETH
> (whispering)
> Dude! She's havin' a fuckin' party.

ANGLE ON: Fogell entering the room

> SETH (CONT'D)
> (whispering)
> Don't tell Fogell about the party.

> FOGELL
> Hey guys, I was walking here, and on the way, I saw Nicola, and she was wearing these tight white pants and a black g-string and you could see it right through the pants.

INT. HALLWAY (FLASHBACK) – EARLIER

We see Fogell, looking at the ass of NICOLA, an incredibly hot girl who exudes sexual vibes and looks a little skanky; you can see her black g-string through her tight white pants. She turns and notices Fogell. He gives an awkward look.

> FOGELL
> It's nine thirty.

> NICOLA
> What?

INT. FOODS AND NUTRITION ROOM (PRESENT) – CONTINUOUS

Back to Fogell, Seth and Evan.

> FOGELL
> I told her what time it was. It was awesome. She's got the nicest ass.

> SETH
> Like you'd know what to do with it.

> FOGELL
> Ha ha. I'm really gonna miss your knee-slappers when me and Evan are at Dartmouth.

SETH
(pissed)
Yeah, well I'll be at Junior college where the girls are half as smart, and thus twice as likely to put me in their mouths.

FOGELL
What are you guys doing tonight?

EVAN
Uh. . .

Seth stares down Evan.

EVAN (CONT'D)
Nothing. As yet.

FOGELL
Well, if nothing comes up we can get shit-faced. Seth always said I was too much of a pussy to do it, but he was wrong. It's been arranged. At lunch, I'm going to the same place Mike Snider went to pick up my brand new fake ID.

SETH
Whoa! No Shit? 'Cause, Evan, didn't you just say that you heard about a party? Now you can buy us booze. Awesome.

FOGELL
Whoa. Nice. Gonna get our drink on.

MRS. HAYWORTH(O.S.)
If you're not in this class, leave this class!

EVAN
Well done, man. We'll see you after class.

Fogell leaves.

SETH
Did you tell that nimrod you're not going to room with him next year?

EVAN
Uh. . . no, not yet.

SETH
You better. You spend too much time with that freak as is.

Evan is clearly bothered by this comment. Seth sees Jules coming.

JULES
Seth, dishes time. What's the hold up?

SETH
We're getting a fake ID.

JULES
Well, you two have four more years to cuddle, so let's get to work.

EVAN
Actually, we're going to different schools.

JULES
Really? You're cutting the cord? What's going to happen?

SETH
Nothing! Jesus. What do people think is gonna happen? That's what I don't get.

EVAN
We're not, like, dependent on each other. We met when we were 8, we were fine before then. It's not like we do everything together.

SETH
Yeah. Now Evan, I've gotta go take a piss. You gonna come hold my dick for me, or what?

Jules laughs.

INT. CLARK SECONDARY CAFETERIA – DAY

Seth and Evan are eating together.

EVAN
So it looks like we get a little graduation party after all. Thank god.

SETH
I would do terrible things to get with Jules tonight. Unforgivable things.

Superbad

                    EVAN
          I hear you. I'd give my left foot to start dating
          Becca.

                    SETH
          Ah, Becca's a bitch.

Evan slams his fist on the table.

                    EVAN
          I'm fuckin' sick of this shit, man! Seriously.
          Why do you hate her? Is there even an actual
          reason? Because seriously, I'm beginning you
          think you like her.

                    SETH
          Hell no! I hate her.

                    EVAN
          Why?

                    SETH
          Fine. Here it comes.
              (beat)
          I was never going to tell you this story, because
          I knew that if you heard it you would never
          want to get with Becca, but you have a right
          to know.
              (beat)
          Well, in the third grade, I had. . . like. . . an
          odd problem. It's not even that weird, really.
          Something like eight percent of kids do it,
          but, anyways—
              (beat)
          For some reason, I don't know why, I used to
          have this thing. . . where I would. . . like,
          kinda. . . sit around all day and draw pictures
          of dicks.

                    EVAN
          What?

INT/EXT VARIOUS LOCATIONS

FLASHBACKS of YOUNG SETH (age 10). In a playground, he sketches a dick in his composition book. In his bedroom, he leans over a text book, drawing phalluses on the founding fathers. MONTAGE of Young Seth drawing dicks in crayon, water-color, pencil crayon, felt marker, etc. We end on a C/U of a dick being drawn with a ball-point pen. REVEAL we are in a classroom.

                    SETH (V.O.)
          I'd just sit there for hours on end drawing dicks.
          I don't know what it was. I couldn't touch the
          pen to paper without it drawing a penis.

                    EVAN (V.O.)
          That's fucked.

                    SETH (V.O.)
          No shit that's fucked up. Here I am this little
          kid who can't stop drawing dicks to save his life.

INT. CLARK SECONDARY CAFETERIA – PRESENT

                    EVAN
          What does that have to do with Becca?

                    SETH
          Just listen.

INT. RANDOLPH ELEMENTARY CLASSROOM – FLASHBACK

Young Seth is still sitting at his desk drawing penises.

                    SETH (V.O.)
          I was very secretive about this dick thing I had
          going, after all, even I thought I was a loon, lord
          knows what other people would have thought.
          So I would take all my dick drawings and stick
          them in this Muppet lunch-box I had.

We see Young Seth sticking a picture of a penis in a lunch-box filled with pieces of paper.

INT. RANDOLPH ELEMENTARY CLASSROOM – DAY

Young Seth is drawing, however it is a different day.

                    SETH (V.O.)
          So one day I was finishing up a picture of a real
          big and veiny bastard, when all of a sudden. . .

Young Seth drops the picture of the dick off his desk. It floats down and hits the feet of a cute little girl, YOUNG Becca.

Screenplay

73

Superbad

INT. CLARK SECONDARY CAFETERIA – PRESENT

          EVAN
    You hit Becca's foot with your dick?

INT. RANDOLPH ELEMENTARY CLASSROOM – MOMENTS LATER

The little girl picks up the picture and looks at it with a truly disturbed look on her face. Young Seth grabs the picture from her and shoves it into his lunch-box.

INT. CLARK SECONDARY CAFETERIA – PRESENT

          SETH
    Well she fucking flipped. She started crying and
    shit. Ratted me out. The principle finds my cock-
    Muppet lunch-box, and *he* fucking flips.

INT. RANDOLPH ELEMENTARY PRINCIPAL'S OFFICE – DAY

A FLASHBACK of Young Seth sitting in the principal's office. The Muppet lunch-box is open and the penis drawings are completely covering his desk.

          SETH (V.O.)
    It turns out the principal was some crazy
    religious guy and he thought I was possessed by
    some dick devil or something.

The principal puts his hand on Seth's head and begins praying for his soul.

INT. CLARK SECONDARY CAFETERIA – PRESENT

          SETH
    So, he calls my parents and they make me go to
    a psychologist who kept asking me all these dick
    questions. My parents wouldn't even let me eat
    dick-shaped foods for, like, months! No carrots,
    no Pop-sicles, no hot-dogs. You know how many
    fucking foods are shaped like dick?

          EVAN
      (half amazed, half amused)
    Wow. That's really messed up. And really gay.

          SETH
    I can't even stand to look at her punk face.
      (beat)
    Let's go get dessert.

Evan looks at his watch.

          EVAN
    I can't. I have to meet with the counselor so I
    can start picking out my classes.

          SETH
    So, what? Now I gotta eat dessert alone like
    Stephen Glanzberg?

Seth motions towards a sad kid eating dessert alone.

          EVAN
    Yeah. What do you want me to do?

          SETH
    Nothing, I guess.

          EVAN
    Relax. I'll see you later.

Evan walks off. Seth is not happy. He looks around the room at all the other kids chatting, eating, and messing around.

Seth stares at a table of kids all laughing together, then gets up and walks out of the cafeteria.

EXT. CLARK SECONDARY WALKWAY – CONTINUOUS

Just as Seth turns the corner he sees Jules, Becca, Nicola, and SHIRLEY standing together. Jules spots Seth.

          JULES
    Seth. There you are.

Jules turns and says goodbye to Becca and Nicola, who leave. Jules and Shirley turn to meet Seth.

          SETH
    Hey. Here I am.

          JULES
    So you're coming to my party, right? It's
    fully on.

          SETH
    Yeah. Why? Should I not?

Screenplay

JULES
No, no, no. I really want you to come. But. . . uh, you did say you were getting a fake ID or something, is that right?

SETH
Very right. Right. I'm getting that.

SHIRLEY
Can you get us drinks?

SETH
Ummm. . . I don't know. I. . . think. . . maybe.

JULES
(half joking)
Come on, you scratch our backs, we'll scratch yours.

SETH
Heh. Well, funny thing about my back. It's located on my cock.

Seth laughs too hard. Shirley is offended. Jules laughs a little.

SETH (CONT'D)
Ha! Alright, sure. I can do that. What do you guys want?

JULES
Well, this is actually, like, a big favor, but, well, my parents gave me like a hundred bucks to feed myself for the week, but the house if full of food, so I figure I should just spend all of it on extra drinks for the party.

SETH
Wow. I would never even think of doing something that nice.

Jules hands Seth a hundred dollars.

JULES
Well, this is really nice of you. I mean, I really appreciate this.

Seth can't believe what he's hearing. He can barely contain his smile.

SETH
Should I just get, like, a shitload of different shit?

JULES
Whatever shit you think people would like, I don't really know.

SHIRLEY
I want Kyle's Killer lemonade.

JULES
Okay. I'll see you tonight.

SETH
Yeah! I'll see you!

The girls walk off, leaving Seth lost in thought. He starts walking quickly down some nearby stairs.

EXT. SCHOOL FIELD – MOMENTS LATER

Evan is standing alone amidst the rest of his gym class as they play soccer.

GYM TEACHER
Evan, get into the game.

Evan says nothing and the teacher soon redirects his attention elsewhere. Evan sees Seth jogging towards him.

SETH
(out of breath, worked up)
Man, just – Evan, listen to me. You know Jules? Her and her stupid friends came up to me and asked me if I would buy them alcohol. Not just her, her whole party. Do you know what that means? It means that by some miracle, we were paired up, we talked, and she actually thought of me afterwards. Thought of me enough to decide that I was the guy that she was going to trust the fun-ness of her party with. She wants me! She fucking wants my dick!

EVAN
Did you ever think maybe she's just using you to get her alcohol?

SETH
Of course I thought of that! LISTEN TO THIS!

Superbad

INT. FOODS AND NUTRITION ROOM (FLASHBACK)

The same scene as before with Seth and Jules in class.

> JULES
> I'm used to it. My older brother always says, like, the nastiest shit. He called me Hymen until I was twelve.

EXT. SCHOOL FIELD – PRESENT

> SETH
> She has an older brother! She could have asked him, but she asked me! She looked me straight in the face and asked me. She wants to fuck me, man. Do you understand that? Fucking! Today is the day that fucking has become possible.

> EVAN
> Are you stupid? You're not going to be able to sleep with her tonight.

> SETH
> She's going to be at the party, Evan. She's gonna be drunk, and she likes me at least a little, so I can get with her. Make out at the very least. Two weeks, hand job. Month, blow job. Then, I make her my girlfriend, and I've got, like two months of solid sex. By the time college rolls around, I'm the fuckin' fucking master!

> EVAN
> Make her your girlfriend? Masterful.

> SETH
> Seriously, once I've gotten with her, I write her love letters, flowers, I'll do anything — I'll be the most pussy-whipped guy in the universe — what chick wouldn't go out with a guy like that?

The soccer ball rolls towards them. They both watch as it rolls by.

> CLASSMATE
> What the hell, Evan? We're down by two points.

Evan shrugs back.

> CLASSMATE (CONT'D)
> Fuck you, man.

> SETH
> Fuck off, Greg. Why don't you piss your pants again?

> CLASSMATE
> That was, like, eight years ago, asshole!

He runs off.

> SETH
> (to Evan)
> Wanna hear the best part?

> EVAN
> (sarcastic)
> Oh, I haven't yet?

> SETH
> Becca!

Evan looks upset, assuming that Seth is about to trash-talk Becca, as usual.

> SETH (CONT'D)
> You do the same thing, man! Buy Becca her alcohol. Then, tonight, when you guys are both drunk, get with her! This is the last party we're ever going to go to as high school people! I've fully ignored my hatred for Becca in coming up with this. I'm flexing nuts. We need to stop being pussies and for once just goes balls out, man!

Evan seems to be swayed.

> EVAN
> I should get Becca alcohol?

> SETH
> Of course! It'll be pimp, and then you know she'll be drunk.

> EVAN
> Have you talked to Fogell?

> SETH
> You talk to Becca, I'll find that retard Fogell.

Screenplay

INT. HALLWAY – LATER

Everyone is rushing to class. Evan hurries through the halls and finds Becca at her locker.

          EVAN
Hey Becca! Hold up. Did you hear about the party tonight?

          BECCA
Yeah, I just heard. It sounds sweet. You're not coming, are you?

          EVAN
No, no, I am. That's why I came looking for you. Me and some guys are going to the liquor store after class, so I was thinking I could buy you yours, if you needed someone to.

          BECCA
Yeah! That'd be great, that'd save me such a hassle, cause I was going to beg my sister, but yeah, could you get me, like, a bottle of Goldslick vodka?

          EVAN
Hey. Is that the one with the little gold flakes in it?

          BECCA
Yeah. I'll pay you back tonight.

          EVAN
You will absolutely not. I refuse. It's my treat.
            (beat)
The first of many.

          BECCA
Wow. Thanks, Evan.

Evan swings a friendly little punch at Becca's shoulder, but someone walks into him, causing him to nail her in directly in the tit!

          BECCA (CONT'D)
Hey!

          EVAN
            (mortified)
I'm sorry! Shit, shit. I'm so sorry! I just wanted to give you a friendly nudge in the arm, you know? I'm sorry.

          BECCA
            (giggling)
Don't worry about it. I'll see you then.

Becca starts walking away.

          EVAN
I'm so sorry about that.

EXT. CLARK SECONDARY – FRONT OF SCHOOL – DAY

Seth is waiting angrily in front of the school. Evan comes out the front doors.

          SETH
Where is that sack of shit? He said he'd be back after lunch, and here I am with my thumb up my ass. Fuck.

          EVAN
I did it, dude. I even offered to pay for it. It was pimp.

          SETH
Whoa. That is fucking pimp. Why didn't I do that? Shit.

The bell rings.

          SETH (CONT'D)
Shit! We're screwed!

INT. WOODSHOP CLASS – CONTINUOUS

Seth and Evan work side by side in the woodshop.

          SETH
            (yelling over the machines)
That's what we get for trusting Fogell! I bet he pussied out, just like I said he would!

EXT. CLARK SECONDARY – AFTER SCHOOL

Seth and Evan walk.

          SETH
I mean, what are we going to tell the girls? "Sorry, we couldn't do what we promised

because we're dick-less incompetents!" We'll never get laid because of that little ass-fuck. How did he get in to Dartmouth?! He's got shit for brains! Shit! How else can we get liquor?

FOGELL (O.S.)
Hey guys!

Seth and Evan turn around to see Fogell running after them.

EVAN
Where have you been?

SETH
Yeah! You almost gave me a goddamn heart attack! You better fucking have it, where is it?

FOGELL
Chill, man. I got it. It's flawless! It's great. Look.

Fogell reaches into his pocket and pulls out the fake ID. Evan grabs it.

EVAN
(reading the card)
Hawaii. Okay. That's good. Hard to trace. . .
(beat)
Mr. . . "McLovin"? What kind of a stupid name is that? What are you trying to be, an Irish R&B singer?

FOGELL
Well, they let you pick any name you want when you get there.

SETH
So you picked McLovin?

FOGELL
It was between that or Muhammad.

SETH
Why was it between that or Muhammad? Why didn't you just pick a common name?

FOGELL
Actually, Seth, Muhammad is the most commonly used name on earth. Read a fucking book.

EVAN
Have you ever actually met a guy named Muhammad?

FOGELL
Have you actually ever met a guy named McLovin?

SETH
No! That's why you picked a bad name.

EVAN
You probably have federal agents tracking you for even considering the name Muhammad on a fake ID! Don't you watch "24"?

SETH
Look at this shit man, you don't even have a first name. It just says "NAME: MCLOVIN"

EVAN
One name? Who are you? Cher?

FOGELL
McLovin sounds old, okay? And chicks'll dig it. Are you kidding me?

EVAN
Under what circumstances would you ever have to show a chick your ID?

FOGELL
She could ask. Or, I could just show it to her.

SETH
Holy shit! I don't believe this. This says you're fucking 25! Why didn't you just put 21?

FOGELL
I knew you would ask that. But listen, asshole, everyday hundreds of kids go to the liquor store with fake IDs that say they're twenty-one. Just how many twenty-one year olds are there in this town? It's called strategy, okay?

SETH
Fool!

Screenplay

Superbad

EVAN
Calm down! It's not terrible! This might work, but it's up to you, Fogell. They'll either think, "Oh, it's another punk kid with a fake ID." Or, "Look, it's McLovin, the twenty five year-old Hawaiin organ donor". What's it gonna be?

Fogell takes a deep breath.

FOGELL
I am McLovin.

SETH
You're not McLovin. No one's McLovin and this is never going to work. We need a new way to get booze. Could we drive to Canada?

FOGELL
It'll work, dumbass. Try not to have a heart-attack.

They walk into the staff parking lot. Seth stops.

SETH
What the fuck? Where's my car?

EVAN
I told you, man! What did I say? I told you that was a dumb idea.

FOGELL
Why would you park in the staff—

SETH
Shut up, Fogell.

FOGELL
'Cause you're not staff.

SETH
I am aware of that, Fagell.

Seth storms off. Evan follows him.

FOGELL
(yelling)
Will you still pick me up from work?

Evan and Seth round the corner, leaving Fogell behind.

SETH
Let's go to your house.

INT. EVAN'S BEDROOM – SOON AFTER

Seth puts on a shirt that is way too small and he's wearing pants that are too tight. Evan is playing the video game Grand Theft Auto.

SETH
Now we wait for your Mom to piss off and steal your parents' booze like your brother always does. Take a bit from every bottle. Piece of cake. It's not exactly what Jules wanted, but it's enough to get a bunch of people shit-faced, right?

EVAN
Come on! Just wear what you wore to school.

SETH
I told you I can't do that, Evan. I can't let Jules see me in the same shit I wore at school. It's completely unbecoming.

EVAN
Why don't you just go to your house and get your own clothes? 'Cause this is stupid.

SETH
You're stupid! I can't go home. Then my mom will know the car got towed and I'll be grounded tonight. I'll just stay here all weekend and pick it up on Monday.

EVAN
(RE: video game)
Where the fuck is the M-16?

SETH
Don't you have bigger clothes? Look at me! I'm never going to get laid in this.

EVAN
See what my dad has.

INT. EVAN'S HOUSE – PARENTS ROOM – SOON AFTER

Seth is wearing Evan's Dad's clothes: a 70s style cowboy shirt, just barely pulling it off, as well as slacks.

Screenplay

                    SETH
        Not bad, huh? Kind of look like one of The
        Strokes.

                    EVAN
        It's, like, 7:30 and my Mom's still here.

                    SETH
        Alright, here's what we'll do. You steal the
        liquor, while I cause a distraction by fucking
        your mom's tits in the basement.

                    EVAN
        Enough, man. Let's just sneak down there and
        grab it.

INT. EVAN'S HOUSE – LIVING ROOM TO KITCHEN – DAY

Evan's Mom is on the phone in the TV room. WE TRACK OVER TO THE DOORWAY to reveal Evan and Seth clandestinely emptying two liter soda bottles into the kitchen sink. They finish. Evan cautiously sneaks a peak at his Mom. She's still on the phone. He gives Seth the thumbs up and quietly leads him into the adjoining den.

INT. EVAN'S HOUSE – DEN – CONTINUOUS

The boys enter and cautiously open the liquor cabinet. Evan grabs a bottle and begins unscrewing the cap, when he notices a little black line marking where the liquor bottle is filled to. Then, he realizes that every bottle is marked.

                    EVAN
            (whispering)
        I can't believe it. They marked them.

                    SETH
            (whispering)
        What do you mean they. . . oh, man! Fuck! Fuck
        them! Your parents are such dicks.
            (beat)
        Actually, just your dad's a dick. Your mom's
        awesome 'cause of her giant tits.

                    EVAN
            (whispering)
        Shh!!! It's fine. We take a bunch of booze and
        then replace what we took with water until it's
        back at the mark, right? I'll get water.

Evan hurries off. Seth looks at the liquor cabinet, trying to choose the best booze. He grabs a massive bottle of gin. Evan reappears.

Evan holds an empty Coke bottle as Seth shakily pours the gin in. Evan starts refilling the liquor bottle with water, when suddenly they both hear his mom coming.

                    EVAN (CONT'D)
            (whispering)
        Fucking, run!

                    SETH
            (whispering)
        But, the booze?

                    EVAN
            (whispering)
        Take it!

Seth runs off with the gin and Coke bottle. Evan quickly closes the cabinet and sneaks off right before his mom enters. Through the window she see's that Seth is already on the front lawn and thinks nothing of it.

                    EVAN (CONT'D)
        Bye, Mom! Love you.

                    EVAN'S MOM
        Love you, sweety.

Evan leaves.

EXT. EVAN'S HOUSE – FRONT LAWN

Evan and Seth triumphantly walk away. Seth holds up the gin.

                    SETH
        Look at this mother. Smell her glory.

He opens it up and takes a whiff.

                    SETH (CONT'D)
        Mmm. It's good. Barely any scent.

He takes a crazy big swig.

                    SETH (CONT'D)
        See that? I always said I had the highest alcohol
        tolerance. I'm like Superman.

Seth taste another swig, but makes a strange face. Evan grabs the bottle and takes a swig.

Superbad

                    EVAN
It's water!

                    SETH
Water?
          (drinks again)
Your brother beat us to the punch. We have to
go back!

                    EVAN
We can't go back! She totally knew, she'll bust
us for sure, and we have to meet Fogell.

                    SETH
Man. I gotta be honest. This is just really
upsetting to me. Are you sure we can't go back?
There's a forty of rum just sitting there.

                    EVAN
We can't. She's savvy.

                    SETH
Well, fuck. . . fine. Text your brother he's a
stupid piece of crap.

                    EVAN
Totally.

Evan whips out his cell and chuckles as he rapidly types.

EXT. GOOD SHOPPER – DAY

Evan and Seth walk off the bus. They see Fogell walking towards them.
He's dressed nicely, wearing a vest.

                    SETH
What the hell is that?

                    FOGELL
A fucking vest, dumbass.

                    SETH
You look like Pinocchio.

                    EVAN
What? It's just a vest.

                    FOGELL
Yeah. How many high schoolers you see in
vests? Try, none.

                    SETH
          (eyeing Good Shopper)
You know, they've got a ton of liquor right in
there. If we get it now we can get to the party
faster with all of Jules' shit.

                    FOGELL
No way! I work there. They know I'm not
twenty-five.

                    SETH
Nobody said anything about you, dick-mouth.
You have one name on your ID. It's out of the
equation! And now I'm gonna have to take
drastic measures.
          (beat)
I'm gonna steal the booze.

                    FOGELL
What?! No! Hell no! You can't do that!

                    EVAN
          (mocking)
Yeah, right!

                    SETH
And then I can give Jules back her money, like
you did with Becca. That was good thinking,
that's fucking pimp. That's how you seal a deal.
It won't be hard. I heard Dan Vertlieb stole a keg
from here and he's like, a fuckin' idiot, and he
got away with it.

                    FOGELL
No! You can't steal it! You can't do that, I work
there!

                    EVAN
You're not gonna steal it. Fogell, he's not going
to steal it.

                    FOGELL
Please. Don't do this! I promise. I'll get the liquor
later. Snider's ID always works, Seth. So will mine!

                    SETH
Snider's ID doesn't have one fucking name,

asshole. I thought you "Dartmouth" boys would
be smart enough to understand that.

Seth walks to the store. Fogell seems nervous, Evan pats him on the back.

                    EVAN
          Don't worry, man. He won't do it.

Fogell suddenly gets excited.

                    FOGELL
              (enthusiastically)
          Hey! I forgot to tell you, my Mom said we can
          have the TV from the basement and I've got,
          like, three lava-lamps and one strobe light, so
          like, we can have that in the room—

                    EVAN
              (nervously)
          Shh. He might hear.

                    FOGELL
          You still didn't tell him we're rooming together?

                    EVAN
          Fogell. Shut the fuck up. We can't have three
          lava lamps. How cliche can you be?

INT. GOOD SHOPPER – DAY

Seth enters the store, looking determined. He spots a SECURITY GUARD standing by one of the registers.

                    SETH
              (to himself)
          Hope piggy can run.

He walks past the registers, which brings him in front of the long liquor aisle. He surveys the scene. There is an OLD WOMAN browsing the shelves. Seth looks over to the registers.

INT. GOOD SHOPPER (FANTASY) – DAY

Seth is at the cash register. He has a huge amount of booze in the conveyor belt.

                    CASHIER
          How old are you?

                    SETH
          Twenty two.

                    CASHIER
          You certainly are. That'll be eighty dollars.

Seth hands the cashier a big EIGHTY DOLLAR BILL.

                    SETH
          Thank you kindly.

                    CASHIER
          You're welcome, Seth.

INT. GOOD SHOPPER – DAY

Seth, still standing in front of the liquor aisle, shakes his head. He eyeballs the old lady.

INT. GOOD SHOPPER (FANTASY) – DAY

The old lady is browsing. She drops her big purse. A hand reaches down and picks it up. It's Seth.

                    SETH
          Excuse me, ma'am. You dropped your purse.
          Would you like me to help you with your
          groceries?

                    OLD LADY
          That would be lovely, young man. Would you like
          me to buy you alcohol?

                    SETH
          That would be lovely!

INT. GOOD SHOPPER (FANTASY) – MOMENTS LATER

Seth, holding two huge bags of liquor, waves to the Old Lady as she pushes a shopping cart toward the door.

                    SETH
          Enjoy your remaining years!

                    OLD LADY
          I will. Enjoy fucking Jules!

                    SETH
          Haha. Okay!

INT. GOOD SHOPPER (FANTASY) – DAY

Seth shakes his head. He looks down the aisle again, takes a breath and starts walking. He arrives at a fancy looking bottle. He takes it and looks down at it in his hands. A big golden label reads, "GOLDSLICK VODKA." Gold flakes swirl around in the bottle.

> SECURITY GUARD (O.S.)
> Don't do it kid.

We see that the Security Guard is right behind him. Seth doesn't look up, he just stares at the bottle dramatically.

> SETH
> I never had a choice.

He throws the bottle at the guard. The guard catches it, then hurls it right back at Seth. Seth dodges it by an inch; the bottle hits the OLD LADY in the head.

> OLD LADY
> (in agony)
> AAAHHHHH!!!

The broken end of the bottle spins across the floor. Before Seth can do anything, the guard picks up the jagged bottle neck and SWINGS it at Seth, cutting Seth's throat. Blood spurts out his neck as he desperately tries to talk.

> SETH
> (choking on blood)
> Haja... blah... blarr..kalla... balagala...

Seth drops his bottles and falls to the ground

EXT. GOOD SHOPPER – DAY

Seth quickly exits the supermarket, looking pale.

> FOGELL
> (to Seth)
> So, where's all the stolen liquor, Danny Ocean? Did you hide it up your ass?

> SETH
> Fuck you! I was gonna do it, but security was tight as shit. I was gonna do it though, don't think I wasn't. Let's go to the liquor store and watch your stupid ID get rejected.

Seth heads towards the bus stop.

> FOGELL
> Wait! I'm gonna put my vest back in my locker!

INT. BUS – DAY

MORE MIND-BLOWINGLY BADASS FUNK MUSIC OVER Seth, Evan and Fogell sitting on the bus amidst a bunch of gloomy, unpleasant looking strangers. Nothing happens whatsoever.

EXT. LIQUOR STORE – DAY

The bus stops in front of the liquor store and the guys get out.

> EVAN
> Well, here we are. Fogell, are you ready?

> SETH
> Here's the list.

> FOGELL
> A list? Why?

> SETH
> We're getting girls their booze so they'll get with us. I put a lot of thought into that list. It's the perfect party bar, so don't mess it up and get Sambuca again.

Fogell reads the list. A worried look sweeps across his face.

> FOGELL
> Ouzo, bourbon, spiced rum, Goldslick—

> EVAN
> Goldslick vodka. That's for Becca, so do not forget it.

> FOGELL
> Rasberry vodka

> SETH
> Oh yeah, and and six bottles of Kyle's Killer Lemonade.

> FOGELL
> This is too much. I can't get away with this much!

> EVAN
> What's the difference?

Seth hands Fogell the money.

FOGELL
I don't know, man. I'm getting, like, really nervous.

Fogell starts breathing very hard and making an ODD NOISE while doing so.

EVAN
Are you okay?

SETH
What the hell are you doing?

FOGELL
I don't know if I want to do this.

SETH
What are you talking about? You just promised you would. What is this shit?

FOGELL
What if they turn me down?

SETH
Then we're in the same place that we're in right now!

FOGELL
It's fucking humiliating! Everyone in the store sees them kicking me out. What if they make me put all the liquor back on the shelf? I can't do that!

SETH
This whole thing is bigger than you, asshead! Just go in there and buy the damn alcohol!

FOGELL
What if I don't feel like it anymore?

SETH
Then I will kill you! How's that? If you don't buy the alcohol, I will kill you!

FOGELL
Killing me won't get you any alcohol, jerkoff! I'm the one with the ID!

SETH
Then I will kill you, cut off your ugly face, put it over mine, and buy it my fucking self.

FOGELL
Yeah! You wish you were me. Then you'd be fucking awesome! Peace!

Fogell storms into the store.

INT. LIQUOR STORE – DAY

At first it all seems overwhelming. Fogell is confused, dizzy, and sweating. He steps behind a large beer display and takes a few deep breaths.

CLERK
Hi there.

Fogell flinches, shocked that someone spoke to him. He keeps walking. He nears a mother and her 17 year old SON. As Fogell passes them, the son seems to recognize him. Fogell clearly recognizes the son. Their eyes meet. Fogell looks in the opposite direction.

SON
Fogell?

FOGELL
(weird voice, covering his face)
No.

SON
Yo, Fogell. 'Sup man. What're you doing here?

FOGELL
(weird voice)
Uh. . . nothing. Not Fogell. . .
(whisper)
Shut up, Izen. You don't know me.

IZEN
(knowingly)
Oh, oh. Cool, cool. Good luck.

He puts his head down and quickly walks away. He arrives at the beer and cooler section. Clearly intimidated, he slowly opens a beer fridge. He grabs one beer attached to a six-pack and pulls it forward. The beer comes loose in his hand as the other five fall to the ground, cracking on impact, and spraying beer all over the place. Fogell scrambles to stop the beers from spraying, but soon finds that it is impossible.

FOGELL
Fuck.

A CLERK approaches Fogell.

CLERK
Is there a problem, sir?

FOGELL
Umm, nope, no problem whatsoever.

CLERK
(pointing to the beer on the floor)
Sir, did you do this? On the floor?

FOGELL
(beat)
No.
(beat)
I think it happened. . . before.

CLERK
Are you sure?

FOGELL
I think I would know. And you should clean this shit up. Someone could hurt themselves.

Fogell walks away.

INT. LIQUOR STORE – LATER

Fogell has a shopping cart filled with booze. He gets in line to pay. He looks ahead to the OLD-LOOKING GUY (35) who is currently at the CASHIER (woman) paying.

CASHIER
Um, yes, may I please see some ID?

OLD-LOOKING GUY
No problem. Heh. I haven't been ID-ed in years. Makes me feel young again.

The guy looks through his wallet. Fogell nervously watches.

EXT. LIQUOR STORE – CONTINUOUS

Seth and Evan wait nervously in the parking lot.

SETH
It's a good ID, right? Mike Snider never had a problem. It's fine. Right?

EVAN
Calm down.
(beat)
Did you remember a condom?

SETH
You brought a condom?

EVAN
Yeah, I figured, you know, might as well. I brought one of those little things of spermicidal lube too.

He takes them out of his pocket.

SETH
You asshole! You laughed in my face when I said we'd be having sex tonight.

EVAN
It doesn't mean you shouldn't be prepared. You didn't even bring one?

SETH
No. That wasn't the plan! We had a plan! I can't believe you did that without even consulting me about it!

EVAN
You keep talking about a "plan". I don't really even understand what your plan is.

SETH
Here's my plan – I'm gonna go down on her for, like, hours. She'll love that. She'll want to go out with that. Or I'll dry hump the shit out of her.

EVAN
Okay. But there's no harm in bringing just one little condom.

SETH
And one little bottle of spermicidal lube. That's psycho shit. You can't let her know you brought that! These girls are 18, not dried up old ladies. They're ready to go.

Superbad

> EVAN
> Fine. I won't bring the lube.

INT. LIQUOR STORE – CONTINUOUS

Fogell pushes his stuff up to the Cashier. She looks at him kind of funny.

> FOGELL
> Hello. . .
> (reading name tag)
> Mindy.

She rings up a six pack of Budweiser.

> FOGELL (CONT'D)
> Oh, I love that stuff. Been drinking it for years. I heard they recently decided to start adding more hops.

Fogell just nods kind of proud of himself. She stops ringing stuff up and looks at him.

> CASHIER
> Umm, okay sir, I'm gonna need to see some ID.

> FOGELL
> Really? Haha. Makes me feel young again.

EXT. LIQUOR STORE – CONTINUOUS

Seth and Evan are still pacing outside the store.

> EVAN
> Do you think I could get Becca to do some kind of long distance thing?

> SETH
> No. Only idiots try to do that.

Seth looks as if he sees something in the distance. He stands upright.

> SETH (CONT'D)
> Holy Shit! It's Cary Hutchins!

> EVAN
> I haven't seen her since she switched schools.

> SETH
> She had the biggest tits ever.

Down the block there is a girl walking a dog.

> EVAN
> I heard she had breast-reduction surgery. Her tits must be crazy perfect now.

> SETH
> They were perfect before! Making her tits smaller? That's like me making my nuts saggier. It's slapping G-d in the face.

> EVAN
> Come on, man, she had back problems. And plus, when they reduce them, they totally reshape them. Make them more supple. Symmetrical.

> SETH
> Alright. I gotta see these bastards. Let's check 'em out.

Seth and Evan run off towards the girl.

CUT BACK TO:

INT. LIQUOR STORE – CONTINUOUS

The cashier is still examining the card. She hands it back to Fogell.

> CASHIER
> That comes to a total of $123.59

A huge smile forms on Fogell's face as he pulls out a wad of money and hands it to the cashier. She starts to gather his change when, SUDDENLY, a BIG GUY runs up and PUNCHES Fogell right in the side of the head!!! Fogell falls to the ground. The dude sticks his hand in the open register, grabs a handful of money and runs!

The whole thing is over in a matter of seconds. Fogell is on the ground, dazed and confused.

> FOGELL
> What the shit happened?!

Fogell sees the distressed cashier frantically dialing the police.

Screenplay

                    CASHIER
              (breathing hard)
        I don't believe it. . . I don't believe it. . . .

EXT. UP THE STREET FROM THE LIQUOR STORE – MOMENTS LATER

Seth and Evan walk down the street towards the liquor store.

                    SETH
        She fully looked way better before.

                    EVAN
        But now that she can jog comfortably, she's lost
        a lot of weight.

Evan sees something in the distance.

                    EVAN (CONT'D)
        Whoa. What's this?

They see a cop car with the lights flashing parked outside the liquor store. Seth and Evan cautiously approach the liquor store and look inside. They see two POLICE talking with the Cashier, and Fogell is standing right beside them!

                    EVAN (CONT'D)
        Shit! They busted Fogell!

INT. LIQUOR STORE – CONTINUOUS

The two police, OFFICER SLATER, 30 and experienced, and OFFICER MICHAELS, 25 and learning, are talking to the Cashier. Fogell stands beside them, nervous and afraid.

                    OFFICER MICHAELS
              (to cashier)
        So, did he punch anyone else?

                    CASHIER
              (losing it completely)
        I can't do this, okay!?! I told you, I have an
        exam tomorrow! Can you understand that? A
        goddamn exam!

The cashier breaks down crying and walks off to the back of the store. The officers look at each other.

                    OFFICER SLATER
        Apparently, she has an exam.

They chuckle and then they turn to Fogell.

                    OFFICER SLATER (CONT'D)
              (turn to Fogell)
        So then, son, you're the one that got punched?

Fogell looks down to his bags of liquor at his feet. Then back at the cops. He nods.

                    OFFICER MICHAELS
        Okay, first things first. What's your name?

Fogell looks like his heart is about to explode out of his chest.

                    FOGELL
        My name, it's. . . it's..
              (tripping over his own words)
        Mc..uh. . . McLovin.

                    OFFICER MICHAELS
        McLovin?

                    FOGELL
        McLovin.

The officers both write down some information.

                    OFFICER SLATER
        Cool name. And your first name?

Fogell looks twice as scared.

                    FOGELL
              (thinking on his feet)
        My first one? Oh. . . this again. Well, uh. . .

Behind Fogell, we see Evan and Seth looking at Fogell through the window.

EXT. LIQUOR STORE – CONTINUOUS

Shocked, Seth and Evan walk away from the window. Seth starts to pace in anger.

                    SETH
        I don't believe this bullshit! I can't. . . this isn't
        happening! I didn't even know you could get
        arrested for this shit! WE NEED THAT FUCKING
        LIQUOR!

Superbad

                    EVAN
          Oh my god. Are they gonna take him
          downtown?

                    SETH
          Fuck Fogell! He got arrested! We're on our own.
          We need a new way of getting liquor.
               (realizing)
          AAAHHH!! The money! Fuck! Fuck! Fuck! How
          much money can you get?

                    EVAN
          What are you talking about? Money? What
          about Fogell?

                    SETH
          That doesn't matter anymore. I just lost a
          hundred dollars of Jules' money!

                    EVAN
          We have to help him!

                    SETH
          Help him? What are we gonna do? Bust him out
          of jail? We gonna bake him a cake with a file in
          it? I don't even know where jail is! Fuck Fogell.
          He's fish food. What we need is alcohol, which is
          impossible, because we don't have any fucking
          money!

Seth steps into the driveway leading to the parking lot.

                    EVAN
          Fine. Just. . . calm down. We need to think. We
          need to think.

                    SETH
          Fuck thinking! We need to act!

Suddenly, a car pulls out of the lot going 10 mph and knocks Seth down!!!

INT. LIQUOR STORE – CONTINUOUS

The cops are still talking to Fogell. He looks completely flustered. He's lost his composure.

                    OFFICER SLATER
          So. . . it's just McLovin?

                    FOGELL
          Yeah.

                    OFFICER MICHAELS
          That's bad-ass

                    OFFICER SLATER
          A lot of people have strange names these days.

                    OFFICER MICHAELS
          Chingy. Shakira.

                    OFFICER SLATER
          I once arrested a man-lady who was legally
          named "Pearl Necklace."

                    FOGELL
          It's just. . . I changed my name. I was going to
          be a singer. R&B.

                    OFFICER MICHAELS
          And, how old are you McLovin?

Fogell looks down at the bags of booze again.

                    FOGELL
          I'm twenty five.

                    OFFICER MICHAELS
          Can I see your ID?

Fogell takes his shaking, sweaty hand, sticks it in his pocket, and pulls out his fake ID. He slowly hands it over to Officer Slater. The cops both look at it, then Fogell. Beads of sweat are running down Fogell's face.

                    OFFICER SLATER
          You're an organ donor?

                    FOGELL
          What?

                    OFFICER SLATER
          I didn't want to be one but my wife insisted.

                    OFFICER MICHAELS
          Just like a woman. Even after you're dead, they
          want to tear your heart out.

The officers start laughing. Fogell is shocked. They hand back the ID.

Screenplay

91

FOGELL
Look. I'm really sorry, but I don't really have any information. I didn't see his face.

OFFICER MICHAELS
Are you in a hurry or something?

FOGELL
Uh, yeah. . . I kinda had to catch a bus.

OFFICER SLATER
Where were you going?

FOGELL
Um. . . near thirteenth and Granville.

OFFICER SLATER
We'll take you there, get your information on the way. Sit tight, McLovin.

Fogell is completely dumbfounded.

EXT. LIQUOR STORE – CONTINUOUS

The driver is pleading with Seth and Evan.

DRIVER
I'm so sorry, man! I'm so sorry! I didn't see you at all. Are you okay? Are you okay? I'm sorry, man. Look, what can I do? Are you okay? I mean, please don't report me, we can figure this out, right?

SETH
Why wouldn't I report you?

DRIVER
Because I'll do anything! Please! Anything! Like, literally fucking anything. Name anything.

The driver glances at the cop car.

DRIVER (CONT'D)
You can trust me, cause, I'll be honest, I have a warrant out for a totally non-violent crime, okay? There.

SETH
Well, I need either a bunch of booze or a bunch of cash, or you're going to jail.

EVAN
(quietly to Seth)
What are you doing?

DRIVER
(beat)
Fine. Just take it.

The driver reaches into his pocket and hands Seth some money.

SETH
What is this? It's seven bucks. This isn't enough.

Seth stuffs the money in his pocket.

DRIVER
It's all I have.

SETH
Well, you better do something quick.
(yelling towards the cops)
Ow! My shoulder! It's killing me!! Help!!!

Seth, acting poorly, pretends he's way more hurt than he is.

DRIVER
No! Wait! Okay, you said you want booze? I can get you alcohol. I'm on my way to this party right now. There's gonna be tons of liquor. I will definitely get you plenty.

EVAN
Whoa, whoa, whoa. Hold on. Come here.

Seth goes over to Evan.

EVAN (CONT'D)
What are you doing?

SETH
What? Jules' money is gone, Fogell's out, we've got no other option. Let's go.

EVAN
I don't like this idea at all. That guy's fucking creepy. Just look at him.

SETH
What?

They look at the Driver, who is staring at Evan with a dumb expression on his face.

                    DRIVER
          (to Evan)
     You know a guy named Jimmy? Cause you
     totally look like his brother.

                    SETH
     You promised Becca you'd get her booze. She's
     gonna have a shitty time tonight if you don't.
     That's all I'm saying.

EXT. LIQUOR STORE – DUSK

The Driver's car pulls away with Seth and Evan sitting in the back seat. A few moments later, the cops walk out with Fogell right behind them carrying the bags of liquor.

                    OFFICER SLATER
          (to Fogell)
     Man, that lady just wouldn't stop crying, huh?
     And you're the one that got punched. Did you
     hear her say she has an exam tomorrow? Boo-
     fuckin'-hoo. Am I right?

                    FOGELL
          (afraid)
     Heh. Good one.

                    OFFICER MICHAELS
     Could we have taken her in? Just to scare the
     shit out of her?

                    OFFICER SLATER
     Hah. Probably could have found a way. But a
     good general rule is only take people in you
     want to ride with. And whiny bitches don't
     make that cut.

The cops chuckle as they all get in the cop car.

EXT. DUSK TO NIGHT TRANSITION SHOT

INT. DRIVER'S CAR – NIGHT

Seth and Evan sit in the back seat. The Driver is in the front.

                    DRIVER
     One of you bros could have sat up here with me.

There is an awkward silence, when suddenly Seth starts to wriggle in discomfort.

                    SETH
     Aaah!

Seth fishes his cell phone out of his pocket and looks at it.

                    SETH (CONT'D)
     875-6611?
          (thinking)
     Holy shit. . .

Seth answers the phone.

                    SETH (CONT'D)
     Jules! What's the haps?

                    DRIVER
     Who is it?

INTERCUT WITH:

INT. JULES HOUSE – NIGHT

There are six girls passing two beers in a circle while dancing blissfully to crappy 80s music.

                    JULES
     Seth! Where are you?

                    SETH
     Jules! I just got in a cab and I'm going to the
     liquor store as we speak.

                    JULES
     Awesome. I can't wait for you to get here.

A huge smile sweeps across Seth's face.

                    SETH
     Really?

                    JULES
     Yeah. I think tons of people might show up,
     which is awesome, because I tried to have a
     party last year and nobody came.

                    SETH
     Well, hope they're in the mood to get drunk.

Superbad

                    JULES
          Okay. See you soon.

Seth hangs up the phone, completely elated.

                    SETH
          She called, man! That's insane! She's practically
          begging for it. She said, "I can't wait for you to
          get here."

                    DRIVER
          That sounds like she fully wants it. Where's she
          gonna get it from, huh, my man? You! That's
          who.
                    (beat)
          You guy's on My Space?

Seth and Evan are very weirded out.

EXT. STREET IN FRONT OF PARTY HOUSE – NIGHT

The Driver's car pulls up in front of a house. The three get out.

                    EVAN
          Hey, are you sure that it's cool we're here?

                    DRIVER
          Oh, definitely. I'm essentially best friends with
          this guy. A whole bunch of my buddies are
          coming. Come on!

The Driver runs into the house happily, Seth and Evan following closely behind.

INT. HOUSE PARTY – LIVING ROOM – CONTINUOUS

The boys enter the house and stand by the front door of the huge party. It's in full swing with all sorts of random-looking people. Nobody is under the age of 25.

                    EVAN
          This is something a smart person wouldn't do.

                    SETH
          Whatever. Just act casual. And old. All we gotta
          do is find the booze and haul ass out of here.

As they make their way through the room, a few people give them looks.

INT. HOUSE PARTY – KITCHEN – NIGHT

They enter the kitchen, where Seth spots what they've been looking for. There are big buckets of ice filled with beer, coolers, wine, vodka, everything.

                    SETH
          Holy shit! Let's grab one of these buckets and
          go.

                    MARK (O.S.)
          What the fuck do you think you're doing?

Seth and Evan freeze, thinking they're busted.

                    DRIVER (O.S.)
          What, man? It's nothing.

The boys turn and see that in corner of the kitchen the Driver, holding a phone, is being yelled at by a very intense, intimidating guy, MARK.

                    MARK
          You calling more of your stupid friends again?
          Ya prick. Your fantastic friends?!?

                    DRIVER
          Mark, calm down, okay? Just relax.

                    MARK
          Get the fuck out of my house. I can kill you in
          this house.

                    DRIVER
          Mark, come on. What the heck? Don't be a dick.

Suddenly, Mark grabs the Driver by the back of the neck and drags him out of the kitchen, through the living room and out the door. A group of people follow, including Seth and Evan.

EXT. HOUSE PARTY – CONTINUOUS

The Driver gets pushed out of the door and lands on the front lawn. Seth and Evan watch from the doorway of the house, a group of people in front of them.

                    DRIVER
          Mark! Dude! This is bullshit! Just chi—

Mark steps on the Driver's hand.

                    DRIVER (CONT'D)
            Ahhhh! Fuck!

The Driver takes his hand out from under Mark's foot. He stands up.

                    DRIVER (CONT'D)
            Fuck you, man. I'll fucking do this!

Suddenly, Mark becomes enraged. He takes a big step forward and brutally KICKS the Driver square in the nuts!

The Driver clutches his nuts and falls to the ground.

                    MARK
            Francis, you and your idiot friends stay away
            from me or I'll shiv your ass hard.

Mark kicks some dirt on the driver and then he and his buddies head back into the house. He makes eye contact with Seth and Evan, who quickly duck back into the party.

INT. HOUSE PARTY – SUN PORCH – NIGHT

The frightened boys dash through the living room and hide on the sun porch. They have a hushed discussion.

                    EVAN
            Dude, let's slip out the back.

                    SETH
            Why? Come on, we're here. Let's just hurry up
            and do this.

                    EVAN
            You want to end up like that guy? Not me, I
            need my nuts.

                    SETH
            We need this liquor!

                    EVAN
            You need it! I don't need it. I'm going to tell
            Becca I like her, and then maybe she'll get with
            me; not after I get her stinking drunk.

                    SETH
            Then why haven't you ever made a move, you
            pussy?

                    EVAN
            Because I respect her! I'm not going to put that
            kind of unfair pressure on her.

                    SETH
            These aren't girls, they're women! They need
            our dicks as much as we need their poons – and
            we all love liquor! I don't see the problem!

                    EVAN
            We're leaving, okay? These guys could kill us.
            You want to get killed for liquor?

                    SETH
            You're really gonna bail on me?!

                    EVAN
                (rolls eyes)
            Jesus. . .

Evan walks out the door.

                    SETH
            Okay, okay. . . if that's how you're going to be,
            then I'll get the booze on my own. And you're
            not getting any. And neither is that jerk, Becca!

Seth storms off.

INT. COP CAR – DRIVING – NIGHT

Fogell sits in the backseat. The cops are in the front. There is silence for a few beats.

                    FOGELL
            Um. . . hey. . . uh, officers. I could answer those,
            uh, questions now if you want.

                    OFFICER SLATER
            We get the gist of it. You were buying some beer,
            some guys came in and robbed the place. I don't
            think we're gonna find 'em this time.

The officers start to chuckle. There is a red light approaching. The officers don't even slow down.

                    FOGELL
            It was only one guy.

Superbad

The flip on their siren and casually cruise through the intersection.

> OFFICER SLATER
> Only one guy? You see, McLovin, if it was two guys, we'd have twice the chance of catching one of them, right? Simple mathematics. But when it's just one guy? I mean, how are we supposed to find one guy in this whole city?

> OFFICER MICHAELS
> Yeah, McLovin. You know how many people there are in this city? I have trouble finding people I know. This job isn't like C.S.I. makes it out to be. I used to think there was semen on everything and there was some huge semen database somewhere. There isn't.

> OFFICER SLATER
> On the job, I've run into semen a total of 0 times in my two and a half years.

They approach another red light. One of them hits the siren and they cruise through the intersection

> OFFICER SLATER (CONT'D)
> (turns to Fogell)
> Michaels is only six months in. . . but the force is strong with him.
> (to Michaels in Yoda voice)
> Learning you are, Padawan.

The car radio goes off.

> RADIO
> We have a 245 at East 24 and Montgomery. It's Bailey's Bar and Grill. Car 43, respond please.

Slater picks up the receiver.

> OFFICER SLATER
> Ten-four.
> (hangs up)
> Nice. Ya see, Michaels, when ever there's a call for a bar, you take it. Get at least a free beer out of it.

> OFFICER MICHAELS
> Good fucking call, sir.

They chuckle.

> OFFICER SLATER
> Hey, McLovin. We got a situation at Bailey's. We have to see to that, but we'll drop you off right after. Okay?

> FOGELL
> Um. . . well. . . I kind of have to—

> OFFICER SLATER
> Sit tight.

Michael's hits the siren and they drive off.

INT. HOUSE PARTY – KITCHEN. – CONTINUOUS

Seth is looking in the fridge, which is full of beer. An ENORMOUS GUY nudges Seth aside and sticks his arm in.

> ENORMOUS GUY
> Hey Mark, you want another beer?

Seth quickly walks away from the fridge and goes down the hall.

> MARK (O.S.)
> Yeah. Grab me a Binyon.

INT. HOUSE PARTY – DANCING ROOM

Seth enters a room of people dancing to hip-hop. He notices all the girls are drinking Kyle's Killer Lemonade, and then locates a cooler full of it across the dance area.

He tries to make his way through the sea of dancing. A hot, sorority-type WOMAN (JACINDA) drunk out off her ass dances over to him and starts grinding against his leg. Seth starts to feel rather uncomfortable.

> JACINDA
> You dance hot.

He doesn't know how to react so he tries to go with it, bumpin' and grindin' with the girl.

EXT. STREET – CONTINUOUS

Evan is walking down the street, mad as hell, when, suddenly, he jumps up and starts squirming.

> EVAN
> Whaa! What the. . . oh..

Screenplay

He takes out his vibrating cell phone and looks at the callers name. . .
Becca.

>   EVAN (CONT'D)
>   Oh dude. Oh dude. Oh dude.

He looks intensely at the cell as it continues vibrating.

>   EVAN (CONT'D)
>   Okay. Okay. Here we go. . .

He presses talk.

>   BECCA (O.S.)
>   (through the phone with horrible static)
>   Eva. . . lo. . . . .

>   EVAN
>   Becca? Becca?!? Fuck. Shit, come on. Becca?!?

INT. GABY'S CAR – CONTINUOUS

Becca sits in the SUV with, Gaby, her best-friend, and two other girls. They are a little done up and very giggly.

>   BECCA
>   Evan? Can you hear me?

>   EVAN (O.S.)
>   (through the phone and much static)
>   . . .fuck. . . shit. . . goddamn. . . Becca. . . ass..

The phone cuts out.

EXT. STREET – CONTINUOUS

Evan sees that he has no reception. He looks back at the party, then at his cell phone. He shakes his head and turns back towards the party.

EXT. BAILEY'S BAR AND GRILL – CONTINUOUS

The cops and Fogell get out of the car and walk towards Bailey's. The officers lead Fogell into the bar.

INT. BAILEY'S BAR AND GRILL – CONTINUOUS

As they enter the bar they immediately see a drunken, crazed HOMELESS GUY screaming at a bar tender.

>   HOMELESS GUY
>   Everywhere?!? You didn't see me pissin' anywhere!!!

Fogell quickly sits at the bar by the entrance to the kitchen.

>   OFFICER SLATER
>   Alright, Michaels. I've got your back. Show this rummy how we roll.

Officer Michaels walks up to the Homeless Guy.

>   OFFICER MICHAELS
>   Excuse me! Sir!

The Homeless Guy turns and sees the cops.

>   HOMELESS GUY
>   AAAHHHHH!!!

He runs for the front door!

>   OFFICER MICHAELS
>   Resisting!

Michaels blocks the door and the Homeless Guy rams into him, knocking him onto a table. He falls to the ground.

>   OFFICER SLATER
>   (sarcastic)
>   Good one, Michaels.

Slater runs at the Homeless Guy and chases him into the dining area. The Homeless Guy knocks over a table, which Slater trips over.

>   OFFICER SLATER (CONT'D)
>   Fuck!

>   OFFICER MICHAELS
>   (nervous)
>   Should I shoot him?!?

>   OFFICER SLATER
>   No, you moron!!!

>   OFFICER MICHAELS
>   Don't call me a moron!

The Homeless Guy makes a mad dash for the kitchen, and Fogell is the only one in his way!

Superbad

Screenplay

OFFICER MICHAELS (CONT'D)
Stop him, McLovin!!!

FOGELL
AHHH!!!

The Homeless Guy RAMS straight into him and knocks both of them onto the kitchen floor!!!

INT. BAILEY'S BAR AND GRILL – KITCHEN – CONTINUOUS

The kitchen staff watch in awe as the Homeless Guy wrestles Fogell on the ground.

FOGELL
Ow!!! Please! Stop, you fucking bum!!!

The Homeless Guy gets up, grabs Fogell and HURLS him into a rack of trays! He then turns to run, but SLIPS on a wet spot and SLAMS his head against the ground! The cops burst into the room to find Fogell panting on his knees with the Homeless Guy unconscious on the floor.

OFFICER MICHAELS
McLovin! Nice!

FOGELL
Uh. . . yeah. No problem.

OFFICER SLATER
I am buying you a beer, McLovin!

INT. HOUSE PARTY – DANCING ROOM – CONTINUOUS

An R&B slow jam plays as an exuberant Seth dances with a Kyle's Killer Lemonade in one hand and Jacinda's ass in the other. The dancing becomes increasingly sexual, but as the song ends, Jacinda moves on.

JACINDA
Thanks for the dance.

Seth glances at the cooler and sees one more Kyle's Killer. He grabs it and puts it in his pocket. The bulge is apparent.

INT. HOUSE PARTY – LIVING ROOM

Seth walks into the living room. There are a bunch of GUYS chilling on the couch, who all look at Seth oddly as he enters.

SETH
Hey, wut up?

The guys just nod at Seth and continue to look at him strangely.

GUY 1
What is that? Is that red wine?

Thinking he's busted, Seth quickly covers the bulge in his pocket.

SETH
Uh. . . no. What? I don't know what you're talking about.

GUY 1
That shit you spilled all over yourself, idiot.

SETH
(sincere)
I didn't spill anything on myself.

Seth checks himself to see what the guy is referring to.

SETH (CONT'D)
Oh shit.

On Seth's upper thigh there is a red splotch about the size of a palm of a hand.

SETH (CONT'D)
What the hell is this?

GUY 1
Oh my lord. You were just dancing in there, right?

SETH
Yeah, so?

The guys all burst out laughing.

GUY 1
It's fucking blood.

SETH
Why would I get blood on my leg from—
(beat of realization)
OH SHIT!

The guys start laughing even harder.

> SETH (CONT'D)
> Some girl perioded on my fucking leg!

> GUY 2
> I've never seen that before in my life.

Seth pokes at the splotch.

> SETH
> That is disgusting.

Guy 1 gets up as Seth tries to cover up the mess with his shirt.

> GUY 1
> I gotta show this to Bill.

> SETH
> Who's Bill? Don't show Bill! No! I can't believe this is happening!

> GUY 2
> We should find who did it.

> SETH
> This is un-fucking-believable. I have to look good tonight!

> GUY 2
> Who'd you dance with?

> SETH
> Who gives a shit? Fuck! These aren't even my pants!

INT. HOUSE PARTY – LIVING ROOM

Guy 1 brings six more guys, including the Enormous Guy, into the room. He points out the stain on Seth's pants. All the guys burst out laughing. Embarrassed and fearful of the attention, Seth starts making his way out of the room.

> SETH
> Yeah. It's really funny, huh? Yuk it up, assholes.

Seth works his way through another room full of people, shielding the splotch as best as he can.

> PARTY DUDE
> Dude! Check it out! That guy's having his period!

Another group of people turn and laugh.

> PARTY GIRL
> He looks about the right age! Should have used wings!

> SETH
> (to himself)
> I gotta clean this shit.

He sees a long line of people standing if front of the bathroom door. He spots a staircase and runs down into the basement.

INT. HOUSE PARTY – BASEMENT – CONTINUOUS

Seth enters the empty basement. He sees a sink and runs over to it and turns on the water.

INT. HOUSE PARTY – CONTINUOUS

Evan nervously walks back into the house to look for a telephone.

INT. BAILEY'S BAR AND GRILL – CONTINUOUS

The cops, Fogell, and the unconscious Homeless Guy each sit at the bar with a Binyon in front of them. Slater's radio goes off.

> RADIO
> Calling all units, armed and dangerous man in the vicinity of—

Click. Slater turns his radio down, ignoring the calls.

> OFFICER MICHEALS
> I gotta say, a big turning point for me is when I realized that I had to look in different places. The gym, an art class, you know, shit like that.

> OFFICER SLATER
> I met the Missus at paint ball. Can you believe that? I shot her in the neck, and we just hit it off. And my first wife — who is a whore — where do you think we met? A bar.

The cops laugh.

Screenplay

                    OFFICER SLATER (CONT'D)
            I bet I know your trick, McLovin. You do the
            whole mysterious guy thing, right?

                    OFFICER MICHAELS
            Yeah McLovin, how's it going with the ladies?

The two cops stare at Fogell, putting him on the spot. He scrambles to think of something that sounds old.

                    FOGELL
            Well, officers, it's not the going with the ladies I
            care about, it's the coming.

The cops and Fogell burst out laughing.

                    OFFICER SLATER
            Oh! McLovin in the house!

They down the rest of the beers and get up.

                    OFFICER SLATER (CONT'D)
                (to Bartender)
            We got an important call. No time to pay!

They head for the door, when Michaels stops them.

                    OFFICER MICHAELS
            Actually, we should probably get some road
            beers.

                    FOGELL
            Fuck yeah, we should.

INT. HOUSE PARTY BASEMENT – CONTINUOUS

Seth is scrubbing at the mark on his thigh, but it's not doing much. He stops for a moment to take a breather as he looks around the basement.

He spots a fridge in the corner and walks over to it. As he opens it, a look of awe sweeps across his face. Every shelf is completely filled with beer.

                    SETH
            Jesus's tits!

He grabs as many bottles as he can and starts sticking them in his pockets, when he notices two large jugs of detergent next to the washer. He thinks for a moment, then begins to empty out the detergent jugs.

INT. HOUSE PARTY – VACANT ROOM – CONTINUOUS

Evan peers into a vacant room and sees a telephone. He nervously enters and picks up the phone. He dials.

INTERCUT WITH:

INT. GABY'S CAR – DRIVING – NIGHT

Becca hushes the other girls as she answers her phone.

                    BECCA
            Hello?

                    GABY
            Is it him?

                    BECCA
                (whispering to the girls)
            Shut up.

                    EVAN
            Hey! Becca. Hi. I had bad reception. Are you at
            the party?

                    BECCA
            No, I'm on my way. Are you still coming?

                    EVAN
            Yeah, of course. Um, about your Goldslick...

Evan can hear all the girls goofing around and giggling.

                    BECCA
                (whispering to the girls)
            Shut up.

                    EVAN
            What's going on there?

                    BECCA
            Oh, nothing, I just wanted to make sure you
            were still coming, you know, and that you didn't
            get caught up at a cocktail party or some club.

                    EVAN
            Nope. I'm gonna be there. Full throttle.

                    BECCA
            Well, I can't wait to see you.

Superbad

                    EVAN
          Okay. Bye.

INT. HOUSE PARTY VACANT ROOM – CONTINUOUS

Evan hangs up the phone and a huge smile forms on his face. As he turns to exit, five older, unbelievably drunk DUDES wander into the room.

                    DUDE 1
          They're going to kill that guy, man. That chick's
          boyfriend was pissed.

                    DUDE 2
          Yeah. And he's a beast.

They start pouring a baggy of coke on the table when one of them notices Evan standing in the corner.

                    DUDE 3
          Hey! Was it you? Are you the guy? The kid with
          the splotch on his crotch?

Evan glances down at his crotch. He is confused and horrified.

                    EVAN
          No. What splotch—

                    DUDE 2
          I know you! Guys! I know that guy, he was at
          that party with me.

                    DUDE 4
          Who's he?

                    DUDE 2
          He's Jimmy's brother. The dude with the crazy
          raps, the one I told you about!

They draw the coke into lines as Evan slowly heads for the door.

                    EVAN
          Oh no, that's not me either. Wrong guy, man.
          Sorry.

Dude 3 gets up and blocks the door.

                    DUDE 3
          No. No, that's you, man. You are fully Jimmy's
          brother! How the hell don't you remember that,
          man?

                    EVAN
          Trust me, man. That wasn't me. I don't even
          listen to rap. I like the Doobie Brothers.

                    DUDE 3
          It was you! I know it! Come on! Rap! I've been
          telling these guys about you. Just give them one
          rap. Come on. Rap. Rap.

They start doing the lines of coke. Evan is very afraid.

EXT. PARKING LOT – NIGHT

Fogell and the cops are in the car drinking beer. Slater finishes chugging a beer, picks up the Breathalyzer, and blows into it.

                    OFFICER SLATER
               (reading results)
          Over! Dammit!

                    OFFICER MICHAELS
          Watch this, I'll get it right on the head.

Michaels blows into it.

                    OFFICER MICHAELS (CONT'D)
          Under! Shit. But I feel hammered.

                    OFFICER SLATER
          Puuusssssaaaayyyyyy!!!!

                    OFFICER MICHAELS
          Shut up.

                    OFFICER SLATER
          You suck at everything, rookie!

                    OFFICER MICHAELS
          Everything except covering for your mistakes.

                    OFFICER SLATER
               (motioning to Fogell)
          Hey! Shut up about that.

Fogell blows into the machine.

                    FOGELL
               (reading)
          0.08! Booya! Dead-on, muthafuckas!

The cops slap him five. Fogell sees that the cops clearly like him; his confidence level increased, he takes a chance.

> FOGELL (CONT'D)
> So. . . you guys got guns, huh?

The officers glance at each other.

> OFFICER SLATER
> Yeah. We got guns.

> OFFICER MICHAELS
> I haven't had one for long, but, man, let me tell you – it's like having two dicks.

> FOGELL
> Can I. . . can I hold one? Your gun?

Michaels and Slater look to each other.

> OFFICER MICHAELS
> I mean, if we took the bullets out?

> OFFICER SLATER
> Yeah. Why not?

Slater pulls out his gun and takes out the clip.

> OFFICER SLATER (CONT'D)
> Here.

Fogell takes the unloaded gun and flops it back and forth in his hands, a huge smile gleaming.

> FOGELL
> Wow. I've never held one. Are they hard to shoot?

> OFFICER SLATER
> If you're Michaels they are. He can't shoot worth dick.

> OFFICER MICHAELS
> I don't know. . . I've been spending a lot of time at the range. They got these targets that look like Zombies now. I could whoop your ass.

> OFFICER SLATER
> Yeah?

> FOGELL
> There's clearly only one way to settle this.

INT. HOUSE PARTY BASEMENT – MOMENTS LATER

Seth is finishing pouring the beer bottles into the second detergent jug. There are about thirty empty beer bottles laying around Seth. He tightens the cap, picks up the two detergent jugs, and heads upstairs.

INT. HOUSE PARTY – LIVING ROOM – CONTINUOUS

Seth emerges from the basement and heads towards the front door.

> SETH
> Peace out-tro.

He's inches away from the front door, when suddenly—

> GUY 1
> There! That's the guy!

Seth turns and sees Mark, the guy who assaulted the Driver, walking towards him. He notices Mark has a splotch on his leg, too.

> SETH
> Hey! You got one, too! We're blood brothers.

> MARK
> Shut the fuck up! You're in my house, so answer my questions – what were you doing dancing with Jacinda?

Horrified, Seth scrambles for excuses.

> SETH
> I. . . I didn't dance with her! I don't even dance! Never even tried it!

> MARK
> (point at Seth's splotch)
> Then where did that come from, asshole?

> SETH
> (terrified)
> I don't know! Maybe me and you rubbed up against each other at some point. Or it's ricochet. How am I supposed to know?

Superbad

INT. HOUSE PARTY – VACANT ROOM – CONTINUOUS

The coked-up dudes are watching Evan intensely.

          EVAN
    Okay. . . go!

         EVERYONE
    I'd like to hear some funky dixie-land, pretty momma gon' take me by the hand.

         DUDE 1
    By the hand, please take me by the hand.

         EVAN
    BY THE HAND, PLEASE TAKE ME BY THE HAND.

         DUDE 2
    Pretty momma!

         EVAN
    Come dance with your daddy allll night long.

         EVERYONE
    I'd like to hear some funky dixie-land, pretty momma gon' take me by the hand.

Evan makes a grand gesture and they all stop singing.

         DUDES
    OH!!!/ We did it!/I'm so fucking high!

         EVAN
    Do you guys know "Roxanne"?

SOME GUY bursts into the room.

         SOME GUY
    Yo, guys! There's a fight!

Dude 3 does a line of coke and they all get up together and charge out of the room.

INT. HOUSE PARTY – LIVING ROOM – CONTINUOUS

There is a crowd gathered around Seth and Mark. The Enormous Guy and Mark's friends are gathered beside Mark.

         SETH
    I swear to God it wasn't me!

Evan and the four dudes who were doing coke walk into the room. Evan is shocked to see Seth at the center of so much commotion. Mark notices the detergent bottle in Seth's hands.

         MARK
    And what the fuck is this?

         SETH
    It's nothing. It's detergent.

         MARK
    Yeah. And what are you doing with it?

         SETH
    I. . . uh, I got blood on my pants.

Mark sees the bottle of KYLE'S KILLER LEMONADE in Seth's pocket and takes it out. He looks at it, then looks at Seth with a look of death.

         SETH (CONT'D)
    I brought that from home.

Suddenly, Mark violently SHOVES Seth and throws the beer bottle at his face!!! Seth holds up a detergent jug and deflects the beer bottle.

It flies towards Evan, who ducks, and nails Dude 1 in the head, glass exploding everywhere!!!

         DUDE 1
    AAAHHHHHHH!!! FUCK!!!

Dude 1 clutches his bloody head as the other Dudes charge at Mark! A full on brawl breaks out! Everyone starts fighting! Two of the Dudes beat on the Enormous Guy. They throw him into Evan.

         DUDE 3
    Hold him!

         EVAN
    What?

         DUDE 2
    HOLD HIM!!!

Evan reluctantly holds the Enormous Guy up as the two Dudes pound on him.

ANGLE ON: Seth, cowering in the corner

Mark runs at Seth and is about to punch him, when suddenly Dude tackles him onto the kitchen island! Seth turns and faces Mark's girlfriend, JACINDA.

>JACINDA
>You motherfucker! Why would you do that? Why?

>SETH
>I didn't do anything! You did!

She grabs a lamp, still plugged in, and swings it at Seth. She hits him square in the chest and the light bulb explodes!

>SETH (CONT'D)
>AHH!!!

>JACINDA
>You ruined my birthday!!! You humiliated me!!! Why?!?

>SETH
>Because you used my leg as a tampon!

She charges at him again, arms flailing. Seth scurries around the room, shielding the blows with the detergent bottles.

Evan throws the Enormous Guy to the ground and runs. Evan backs off, spots Seth, and follows him out of the party.

EXT HOUSE PARTY – FRONT YARD

As Seth and Evan run up the block together, Jacinda talks into a cordless phone.

>JACINDA
>Yeah, Fifth and Paysview, please hurry!

EXT. DARK STREET – CONTINUOUS

The cops and Fogell stand beside the car. The Homeless Guy is sleeping in the back. Michaels has his gun drawn and is carefully aiming at a distant stop sign.

>OFFICER SLATER
>You've been saying some bold words, my friend. Better not mess up.

>FOGELL
>You can do it, officer.

BLAM!!! Michaels blasts off a round, which punches a hole right through the center of the "O" in the stop sign.

>OFFICER MICHAELS
>Boo-yaka-sha!!! Suck it, Slater. Suck my nuts. Long, but gentle.

>FOGELL
>Yeah! And eat his ass!

They laugh.

>FOGELL (CONT'D)
>Can I shoot one?

>OFFICER MICHAELS
>Yeah. Sure. Here. Go nuts.

Michaels hands Fogell the gun, when suddenly a SIREN can be heard in the distance getting closer.

>OFFICER MICHAELS (CONT'D)
>Fuck. The cops!

>OFFICER SLATER
>Let's bail! Shotgun!

Slater grabs the gun out of the disappointed Fogell's hand and holsters it. They all hop into the car.

INT. COP CAR – DRIVING – NIGHT

Slater kicks it into drive and they peel out. Fogell shoves the unconscious Homeless Guy over.

>OFFICER MICHAELS
>So, dudes, what do you want to do now?

Suddenly, the car radio goes off.

>RADIO
>We got a 257 at Fifth and Paysview, all units in the area report to Fifth and Paysview. Car 98. That's you. Do it. Seriously.

The cops stop and listen.

>OFFICER SLATER
>Son-of-a-bitch.
>   (picks up radio)
>Car 98, ten-four.
>   (hangs up)
>Ya dumb whore. Ha!

Superbad

Screenplay

FOGELL
What does that mean? We gonna get to shoot anyone?

OFFICER SLATER
I wish. Probably some lame house party. We'll drop you off after. Cool?

FOGELL
Yeah, man. Let's show these fuckers how we roll.

Michaels types some information into the computer.

FOGELL (CONT'D)
So, like, what does that computer do?

OFFICER SLATER
Pretty much anything, if you're smart enough to figure it out. Like, who do you really hate? Gimme a name.

FOGELL
Um. . . my French teacher. Mrs. Daniels. Marie Daniels.

Michaels bring her file up, then punches a few buttons and smiles.

OFFICER MICHAELS
Tomorrow, Mrs. Daniels will have a boot on her car.

Fogell laughs his ass off.

FOGELL
I hate my dad, too!

EXT. NEIGHBORHOOD STREET – MOMENTS LATER

Seth and Evan are running down the sidewalk. They both slow to a stop to catch their breath. The party is nowhere in sight.

SETH
(wheezing heavily)
. . . huff. . . hufff. . . you fuckin' prick. . .

EVAN
What?

SETH
You. . . huff. . . bailed on me. . . huff. . . man.

EVAN
No I didn't!

SETH
Of course you did! We were supposed to do something and you left instead of doing it! That's the definition of bailing!

EVAN
If you said we should burn our dicks off and I didn't, that's not bailing!

SETH
It is bailing, if you promised to burn your dick off!

EVAN
What?!!

SETH
The bottom line is you're a bailer. You just bailed on me, you bailed on me this morning when Jesse spat on me, and you're bailing on me next year!

EVAN
Oh! Okay! There it is! It finally comes out! That's good. Thank you.

SETH
We were supposed to go to college together! Since elementary school! What ever happened to that!

EVAN
What happened to that, is that you're too stupid to get into the schools I did!

SETH
Too stupid? You got into fuckin' Dartmouth. That was never part of the plan!

EVAN
How self centered can you be? Seriously. You were totally good to let Fogell take the fall back there, and you clearly don't like me going to a good school, I mean, what the fuck, man? I. . . I'm not going to let you slow me down anymore.

SETH
What?

Superbad

                    EVAN
        I'll tell you what – you've wasted all my time!
        Instead of chasing girls and making friends, I
        threw away the last three years talking bullshit
        with you! And now, because of you, I'm going to
        college a fucking friendless virgin!

Seth can't believe it. He's extremely hurt.

                    SETH
        Getting with a girl won't make you any less of a
        loser next year!

                    EVAN
        You talking to me or yourself? You fucking
        loser!

Seth drops one of the Tide bottles and shoves Evan hard. Evan shoves him back.

INT. COP CAR – DRIVING – NIGHT

The cop car cruises down a dark street.

                    OFFICER SLATER
        Okay. We should be close. McLovin, are the
        numbers on that side odd or even?

                    FOGELL
        It's too dark out.

                    OFFICER SLATER
        We got flashlights.

Michaels and Slater start making light saber noises and pretend to fight with their flashlights.

                    INT. COP CAR – CONTINUOUS
        Michaels turns and points his flashlight out
        Slater's window, accidentally shining the light
        into his eyes.

                    OFFICER SLATER
        My eyes!

He jerks the wheel.

EXT. SIDEWALK – CONTINUOUS

Seth swings at Evan with the giant detergent jug. Evan dodges it and shoves Seth hard. Suddenly, Seth gets HIT by the out of control COP CAR!!! Seth flies up onto the hood, SMASHING the windshield. The car screeches to a halt and he slides off the car.

Seth lies motionless, still holding one of the detergent jugs. The cap is knocked loose and beer is spilling out.

INT. COP CAR – STOPPED – NIGHT

Everyone in the car is looking forward, stunned. They can't see out the front window, as it is shattered. Fogell has no clue who the victim was.

                    OFFICER SLATER
        Oh shit. Shit, shit, SHIT!

                    OFFICER MICHAELS
        You fucking idiot! What did you do?!

                    OFFICER SLATER
        You shined the fucking light in my face!

                    OFFICER MICHAELS
        Shit! I don't believe this is happening again.

                    FOGELL
            (frightened)
        Oh my god. . . is he. . . are you gonna make
        sure he's alright?

                    OFFICER SLATER
        Okay, okay, we're gonna get out of the car now.
        McLovin, you stay right there.

                    OFFICER MICHAELS
        That guy better not be dead.

EXT. NEIGHBORHOOD STREET – CONTINUOUS

The cops get out of the car and walk over to a now sitting up Seth. He's dazed, but okay. The boys notice the cops.

                    OFFICER SLATER
        Is everyone alright?

                    SETH
            (sarcastic)
        We're great.

OFFICER SLATER
(removing his baton)
Pardon?

EVAN
Nothing.

The cops notice one of the detergent jugs in the middle of a puddle of beer. Slater dips his finger in rubs it against his gums like it was cocaine.

OFFICER SLATER
Pabst. You kids been doing a bit of drinking?

EVAN
No officer. Not at all.

INT. COP CAR – STOPPED – NIGHT

Fogell anxiously sits in the cop car. He can't see what's going on through the shattered windshield. He can overhear the cops talking near the car.

EXT. NEIGHBORHOOD STREET – CONTINUOUS

The cops turn away and start to whisper to one another. Seth and Evan look on, nervous.

OFFICER SLATER
Alright, Michaels. The car is completely fucked, thanks to you—

OFFICER MICHAELS
Thanks to me? You're the one who hit him!

OFFICER SLATER
You blinded me. You've got to fix this!

OFFICER MICHAELS
No way! I did your dirty work last time!

OFFICER SLATER
Goddamnit, Michaels. I don't want to get shit-canned. I like this job.

OFFICER MICHAELS
Me too! I get free haircuts! But I'm not taking the fall again!

Slater looks really pissed. He takes a deep breath.

OFFICER SLATER
Okay, okay... here's what we do. We arrest these little crap stains and dump it on them, I'll take care of that. You go make sure McLovin is good to play ball.

OFFICER MICHAELS
What if he isn't?

OFFICER SLATER
Make him.

Fogell looks terrified He ducks backs as Michaels heads towards his door.

Meanwhile, Slater walks back over to the boys. He pulls out his gun, scaring the shit out of Evan and Seth.

OFFICER SLATER (CONT'D)
Get on the ground. Now! Spread your shit!

Evan and Seth lie down on their stomachs and spread their arms and legs out, terrified.

EVAN
Puh... please don't shoot.

OFFICER SLATER
(mocking)
Puh— Puh— Please shut the fuck up! Spread your shit!

INT. COP CAR – CONTINUOUS

Officer Michaels is sitting in the driver's seat.

FOGELL
W—was the guy alright?

OFFICER MICHAELS
What? Oh, yeah, the guy was fine.

Michaels looks back at the Homeless Guy, who looks a little bit more awake than before.

OFFICER MICHAELS (CONT'D)
Are you awake, sir?

The guy starts to open his eyes a little. Michaels grabs the guy's face and slams it back, knocking him out again. Fogell jumps a little.

OFFICER MICHAELS
I'm sorry, McLovin. But I really need this to be a private thing.

Officer Michaels takes out two cigarettes, and gives one to Fogell, who accepts, quivering in fear. Michaels lights his, then passes the lighter to Fogell.

OFFICER MICHAELS
Listen McLovin, you. . . like. . . Officer Slater and myself, don't you?

Fogell tries to light his cigarette. It takes a few tries and he starts hacking after the first pull.

FOGELL
(coughing)
Umm, yeah, sure. You guys are great.

OFFICER MICHAELS
Good. Now, we're going to arrest these guys, and if you don't mind, which you shouldn't, we'd like you to fill out a little witness report saying they jumped out in front of our car. Cool, McLovin?

Fogell nods his head, getting some of his cigarette smoke in his eyes. He winces and starts to blink in discomfort.

EXT. NEIGHBORHOOD STREET – CONTINUOUS

Slater stands above the boys.

OFFICER SLATER
Now hold hands, boys.

SETH
Uhh. . . why?

OFFICER SLATER
Because you don't want a new butthole where you fucking face used to be! I'm the cops! You listen to me!

Seth nods. Officer Michaels and Fogell get out of the car. Seth and Evan see Fogell and stare in shock as he takes a drag of a cigarette and then flicks it aside.

Michaels pulls Slater aside and mumbles into his ear. Fogell turns and sees Seth and Evan — he's completely dumbfounded!

Evan starts to look really nervous, like he might literally explode. He starts to stand up.

The cops are still talking when suddenly, Evan BOLTS!

OFFICER MICHAELS
Shit!

The cops run after Evan! Seth and Fogell look at each other. Seth grabs the remaining detergent jug and runs off in the opposite direction of Evan! Fogell reaches into the cop car, grabs the bags of booze, and follows Seth.

FOGELL
Seth! Wait up!

Officer Slater looks back to see Seth and Fogell running.

OFFICER SLATER
Shit! Shit! McLovin bailed!
(staring back at the car)
You take the kid!

Slater runs back to the car and looks at the shattered windshield.

OFFICER SLATER (CONT'D)
Dammit!

He takes grabs his billy club and smashes the windshield out.

HOMELESS GUY
What?

The Homeless Guy scares Slater.

SLATER
What the—
(beat)
Get out!

HOMELESS GUY
But I'm arrested.

Screenplay

EXT. NEIGHBORHOOD STREET – NIGHT

Evan is running on a straightaway, Michael in pursuit. We see from the look on Evan's face that he is truly running as fast as he possibly can. He pulls farther and farther away from Michaels, who realizes he can't possibly catch Evan.

>   OFFICER MICHAELS
>   Stop! Stop!
>   (to himself)
>   *Huff* Fast kid.

Michaels slows to a stop as Evan disappears. Michaels drops to his knees, hyperventilating.

EXT. NEIGHBORHOOD STREET – NIGHT

Slater pulls the Homeless Guy out of the cruiser, hops in, and peels out fast.

The Homeless Guy rolls around a bit then stands up. He Grabs the jug of detergent that was left on the ground, and stumbles off.

EXT. NEIGHBORHOOD STREET – CONTINUOUS

Fogell and an exhausted Seth are running together. They hear the cop cruiser coming.

Seth grabs Fogell and takes him around a house and towards a driveway. A second later, a furious Slater drives by the house and continues up the block.

EXT. BACK YARD – MOMENTS LATER

Seth and Fogell sprint into a big, dark backyard. Seth looks back to see if they are being followed. . . BOOM! He runs smack into a little green tent and trips onto it! KIDS inside the tent start screaming as flashlights turn on.

>   KIDS
>   (hysterical)
>   Help/ It's a monster!/ Daddy!

Fogell helps Seth get up. They try to run, but Seth is caught on the tent! He drags it a couple feet as the kids start clawing to get out.

>   KIDS (CONT'D)
>   We're stuck!!! We're gonna be killed by a
>   monster!!!!!!!!!!!

The zipper opens and a KID hops out. The Kid looks at Seth.

>   KID
>   DADDY!!!! MONSTER!!!!!!!!!!
>   FOGELL
>   Holy shit! Little kids!!!

A little GIRL runs out and books it into the house. From inside the tent, another kid starts kicking at Seth.

>   SETH
>   Stop! I mean you no harm!

Seth manages to free himself from the tent and he and Fogell fall to the ground. The kids continue to scream.

>   FATHER(O.S.)
>   Get away from my children!

The guys turn and see a crazed, slightly overweight FATHER in his underwear running at them with a baseball bat. Fogell and Seth scramble to their feet as the Dad takes a swing at them, narrowly missing them.

>   FATHER(CONT'D)
>   You sick sons-of-bitches!

Seth and Fogell run towards a chain-link fence. Fogell puts the bags full of booze over the fence, then hops it. Seth isn't even at the fence yet. He looks back to see the Father coming for him.

Seth swings the detergent jug at the Father, knocking him on his ass. He quickly gets up and charges, enraged. Seth desperately hurls himself over the fence and into the adjoining yard. He runs after Fogell.

Seth coughs and wheezes, slowing down as he lugs the detergent. The Father sees the boys running. He throws his baseball bat. It sails through the air and nails Seth in the back! He falls.

>   SETH
>   Fuck off!

He gets up and the keeps running.

INT. COP CAR – CONTINUOUS

Slater drives, looking for any sign of the kids, pissed as hell. He sees Michaels, crouched over, desperately trying to catch his breath.

Superbad

                    OFFICER SLATER
                Jesus, man!

Slater watches from a distance as Michaels, gasping and wheezing for dear life, pukes.

EXT. NEIGHBORHOOD STREET – NIGHT

Slater pulls up next to Michaels.

                    OFFICER SLATER
                You let him get away?

                    OFFICER MICHAELS
                He's. . . *huff*. . . he's a freak. Fastest. . . oh
                god..fastest kid ever. . .

                    OFFICER SLATER
                Shit. What do we do?

                    OFFICER MICHAELS
                Maybe *huff* I should fire a shot? Scare 'em
                out?

EXT. INSIDE SOME BUSHES – CONTINUOUS

Evan is nestled inside a large bush, frantically trying to reverse his clothes so as to disguise himself. He keeps looking out for the cops, when suddenly he hears a gunshot – BLAM!!!

                    EVAN
                (to himself, mumbling)
                Oh god. Oh god. They shot Seth. I know it.

As he fumbles to turn his jacket inside out and get it on, he sees Seth and Fogell running towards him. He pops out of the bush, scaring Fogell and Seth.

                    FOGELL
                Ahh!

                    SETH
                Jesus!

                    EVAN (CONT'D)
                Should I run!?!

                    SETH
                Yes!!

They all run off down the street.

DISSOLVE TO:

EXT MAIN STREET – NIGHT

Turn onto a main street and are exuberant at the sight of an oncoming bus. It stops at a nearby stop. They haul ass and make it on.

INT. BUS – DRIVING – NIGHT

Out of breath, the boys dig up change and put it in the toll box, then walk towards the back of the bus.

                    HOMELESS GUY (O.S.)
                Hey! It's you! McLovin!

Fogell looks up and sees the Homeless Guy stumbling towards them, sucking back the bottom of the lost detergent bottle. The Homeless Guy sees they have bags full of booze.

                    HOMELESS GUY (CONT'D)
                Well, you little shit. . . ain't got no cop people to
                help you keep your booze. . . gimme it. . .

The Homeless Nutcase reaches for the booze. Seth steps in front of him.

                    SETH
                Back off, or we'll kick the shit out of you!

                    EVAN
                We can't do that. He's homeless.

                    SETH
                So? Who cares? Just because he doesn't have a
                home doesn't mean he doesn't deserve a beat-down.

                    HOMELESS GUY
                Give me the booze!

The guy shoves Seth aside and dives at Fogell.

WE GO INTO VERY SLOW MOTION:

— Becca's bottle of Goldslick gets knocked from the bag. It VERY SLOWLY falls towards the ground.

— Seth reaches for it, but doesn't quite grab it.

— WE LOUDLY HEAR the bottle as it slams against the bus floor. . . but doesn't break! It slowly rises back up into the air and begins sailing towards the front of the bus.

Screenplay

113

Superbad

— Evan LEAPS through the air, sailing towards the precious Goldslick with his arms extended.

> EVAN
> (in slo-mo voice)
> GOOOOOOOLDSSSSLLLLLIIIIIIIICCCCKKKKK!!!!!

— He is inches away from grabbing it, when it suddenly smashes into a pole, SHATTERING, sending little gold flakes everywhere.

BACK TO NORMAL.

The Homeless Guy sees the gold flakes.

> HOMELESS GUY
> Shit!!! Gold!!!

He starts frantically picking up the flakes as Evan stares at the remains, shocked. Fogell walks over.

> FOGELL
> Where the fuck did you guys come from? Have you been following me the whole night?

> BUS DRIVER
> (calling from front)
> Get off the bus or I'm calling the cops!!!

The boys look at each other terrified, and get off the bus.

EXT. BUS – CONTINUOUS

Seth and Evan are looking at one another coldly as the bus pulls away. Fogell looks at some nearby street signs.

> FOGELL
> (ecstatic)
> Holy shit! We're like three blocks away! Best luck ever!

EXT. JULES' PARTY – MOMENTS LATER

They walk up the street towards Jules' as Evan reverses his clothes and puts them back on right-side out.

The guys walk up the front steps of Jules' house. They stand in front of the door.

> FOGELL
> Fuck yeah, guys. We made it. Together and safe.

> EVAN
> I can't believe Becca's bottle broke.

> FOGELL
> I'm sure it'll be fine.

> SETH
> (sarcastic)
> What's the difference? I thought you didn't need it anyways. I thought you were just going to tell her how you feel, you fucking pussy.

> EVAN
> Yeah? Well, good luck getting Jules drunk enough to have sex with you.

> FOGELL
> What's wrong with you guys?

> SETH
> Shut up, Fogell. Never mind. Evan'll tell you next year.

> FOGELL
> (to Evan)
> You told him?

Evan stares Fogell down.

> SETH
> Told me what?

> FOGELL
> Well we have to tell him now.

> EVAN
> Fuck, Fogell! You're a god damn idiot.

> FOGELL
> Well, he knows something's up.

> SETH
> Just say it!

                              EVAN

Shit.

                             FOGELL

Seth, me and Evan are rooming together next
year. What's the big fucking deal? *Oooh. I'm
living with Evan.* Why don't you fucking cry
about it.

                              EVAN

I didn't tell you because—

Seth gives Evan an angry and disappointed look.

                              SETH

Because what? 'Cause you're a backstabber and
you lied to your best friend and you're always
hanging out with Fogell and you just don't care
anymore. I never expected this kind of shit
from you, Evan. Not from you.

Seth just goes into the house with the booze, leaving Fogell and Evan.

                             FOGELL

We never should have had to hide our
arrangement.

INT. JULES' HOUSE – LIVING ROOM – CONTINUOUS

The party is in full swing. There is loud music blaring and nearly a hundred people talking, dancing, and smoking.

                              JULES

Seth! Everyone, he's here! He's got it!

Everyone turns around and sees the Seth holding all the liquor.

INT. JULES KITCHEN

Everyone starts cheering! Seth sets it out on the kitchen table; it is an impressive array of inebriates.

                              SETH

The bar is open!

                            EVERYONE
                      (ecstatically cheering)
Yeah Seth!/Clutch!/Nice!/I can't believe it!/Seth
did that?!/ Who the fuck is Seth?

Jules approaches Seth.

                              JULES

This is awesome. Thank you so much.

                              SETH

Sorry it was late.

                              JULES

Yeah. To be honest, people were starting to
get seriously pissed off. Listen, I've got to go
tell everyone the drinks are here. Don't go
anywhere. Promise?

                              SETH

I'll be right here.

Jules walks off.

INT. JULES' KITCHEN – MOMENTS LATER

Tons of kids pour themselves drinks. Seth and about six other kids all have overflowing shots of Jaeger.

                              SETH

To Jules!

Everyone drinks and recoils from the taste. A random guy refills everyone's shot glasses.

                           RANDOM GUY
                        (pointing to Seth)
Another one, but to you, man! Everyone, to this
guy! Who the fuck are you, man?

                              SETH
                           (exuberant)
Seth!

                           RANDOM GUY

To Seth!

                            EVERYONE

To Seth!

They all drink.

Superbad

                    SETH
          Hey! Let's do another one to me!

Everyone laughs as Seth, very pleased with himself, starts refilling shot glasses.

EXT. JULES BACKPORCH – CONTINUOUS

Evan walks out onto the back porch, looking for Becca. He sees Gaby.

                    EVAN
          Gaby! Hey.

                    GABY
          Where have you been, you almost blew it.

                    EVAN
          What?

                    GABY
          Becca. She's been waiting for you. She's right
          over there. She's been yammering about you all
          night.

                    EVAN
          What? What did she say? Does she think I'm a
          good guy? What did she say?

                    GABY
          It was something like, "I'll fully blow him
          tonight."

                    EVAN
          What?!?

Evan looks over and sees Becca standing on the balcony with a big group of people. He gets really nervous.

                    EVAN (CONT'D)
          Oh man. This is too much. Oh god. What do
          I do? I lost the Goldslick I was supposed to
          bring her!

                    GABY
          Well, Rhea stole some tequila from her parents
          and her and Becca have been going at it. I'd just
          go over there and invite her upstairs, pronto.

                    EVAN
          What? Oh man...

                    (so nervous)
          But... she's totally hammered. If I get with her,
          and I'm not drunk, isn't that, like, unethical?

                    GABY
          It's not unethical if you're drunk, too.

                    EVAN
          I guess.

Evan looks at Becca and takes a deep breath.

INT. JULES BATHROOM – MOMENTS LATER

Evan enters the bathroom and slams the door shut, a bottle of Ouzo in one hand and a beer in the other. He looks at himself in the mirror, seeming as though he's on the verge of a full-on panic attack.

                    EVAN
                    (panting)
          Calm down, Evan. She likes you. She wants to
          suck on your penis. That's a good thing.

He opens the Ouzo and smells it, recoiling in disgust.

                    EVAN (CONT'D)
          Down the hatch.

Evan takes a mighty swig, then gags and spits it out, spraying it everywhere.

INT. JULES' DEN – CONTINUOUS

Fogell sits bored in front of the TV, drinking a beer. He watches a bunch of girls flirt with some boys. Everyone is talking and laughing while he sits alone.

INT. JULES' HOUSE – DANCING ROOM

He walks over to the doorway of a room filled with girls dancing. In the corner dancing is Nicola. He stares at her for a moment, then goes back and sits in front of the TV.

INT. JULES' HOUSE – DEN – NIGHT

He changes the channel and "COPS" comes on the screen. It shows two cops chasing a crack head, tackling him and knee dropping him. Fogell ponders as he watches "COPS." He throws back the rest of his beer and marches into the room Nicola is dancing in.

INT. JULES' HOUSE – DANCING ROOM – NIGHT

He walks up to Nicola, who is by far the best-looking girl in the room, and starts dancing with her. She looks a bit thrown at first, but after a few beats, she seems to like it.

                    FOGELL
          Fogell.
              (beat)
          'Sup.

They continue dancing.

I/E. JULE'S KITCHEN/BATHROOM – CONTINUOUS

MONTAGE INTERCUTTING SETH AND EVAN DRINKING:

INT. JULES KITCHEN

— Seth taking shot after shot in the kitchen with everyone else, glancing over at Jules every now and then as she walks around the party, sending more people to drink with him.

INT. JULES BATHROOM

— Evan in the bathroom, forcing himself to brutally suck back a disgusting amount of Ouzo. He sips from his beer, takes a deep breath, and then starts again.

INT. JULES HOUSE

— Seth dances jokingly with a few people and tells the story of that evening, showing them the detergent jug full of beer and acting out the car hitting him.

INT. JULES BATHROOM

— Evan, who has drank about half the bottle and is pretty drunk, stands up, arms reached out, and tries to walk in a straight line. He does it fairly well. Frustrated, he sits back down and takes another disgusting swig of Ouzo.

INT. JULES HOUSE

— Jules throws Seth a smile when she sees him making everyone laugh as he re-fills their cups with very foamy, slightly blue-tinted beer from the detergent jug.

INT. JULES BATHROOM

— Evan can't keep his balance as he tries to touch his nose while standing on one foot. He's drunk. He drinks from the tap thirstily, eats some toothpaste, fixes his collar and hair, and then gathers his courage, takes a deep breath, and steps out of the bathroom.

EXT. BACKYARD – CONTINUOUS

Evan walks out on the balcony. He spots the circle of people Becca was standing in, only now Becca is laying on the ground, laughing hysterically. Everyone in the circle is looking at her and laughing as well. Evan is extremely nervous. Becca looks up and spots him.

                    BECCA
              (laughing)
          Evan!!! Hey! Come here!!!

Evan takes a deep breath walks up to where she's laying. She extends her arms.

                    BECCA (CONT'D)
          Help me up! None of these people will help me
          up!

Evan notices that she seems a little drunk. He helps her up and she collapses onto him, forcing him to hold her up.

                    EVAN
          Hey, Becca. Sorry I was—

Becca laughs hysterically as she latches onto Evan. He smells her breath. It reeks of alcohol.

Evan's drunk, but Becca is completely fucking shit-faced!

                    BECCA
          Evan! Oh my god! You are so fucking hilarious!
              (to the group)
          Do you goes know how fucking hilarious
          Evan is?
              (to Evan)
          Tell them how hilarious you are!

The group looks over to Evan.

                    EVAN
          Uh. . . well. . . uh. . . hey. What's going on?

                    BECCA
          Listen to him!

Becca starts laughing hysterically.

Superbad

> BECCA (CONT'D)
> See?!! He is so cute!

The group chuckles a little. Becca puts her arms around Evan.

> BECCA (CONT'D)
> I've been waiting for you for, like, ever. What took you so long? Do you have my Goldslick?

> EVAN
> Oh man, it's a crazy story—

Becca picks up a bottle of tequila and shoves it into Evan's hand.

> BECCA
> Here! Don't worry, we can drink this.

> EVAN
> I'm already pretty wasted. But. . . uh. . . here's to you.

Evan takes a much-unwanted drink and gags.

> BECCA
> Light-weight!

Everyone laughs.

> BECCA (CONT'D)
> Hey. . . me and you should go upstairs now. I really want to. . . tell you something.

> EVAN
> (confused and drunk)
> Uh. . . uh. . . uh. . . you could just tell me right here—

> BECCA
> (laughing)
> No! Let's go upstairs, come on!

Evan hears everyone giggle as Becca pulls him towards the house. Becca trips, just managing not to fall.

> BECCA (CONT'D)
> Careful. . .

INT. JULES' HOUSE – DANCING ROOM – NIGHT

Nicola and Fogell are standing in the corner of the room. Nicola is looking at Fogell's ID.

> NICOLA
> McLovin! Wow. What a cool name. So, like, what's Hawaii like?

> FOGELL
> It's fucking awesome. Rainbow state.

INT. JULES KITCHEN – CONTINUOUS

The party is in full swing and everyone is getting good and drunk. Jules walks up to Seth, who is clearly piss drunk.

> JULES
> Hey, I'm back. I had to thank the peeps for comin' out.

> SETH
> (really, really, drunk)
> Jules! The hostess with the most-est! The woman of the hour!

Seth takes a swig of a beer.

> SETH (CONT'D)
> This party's blowin' my ass off! I want you to have a drink with me.

Seth offers her a beer.

> JULES
> No, thanks. I'm good. But, seriously, thanks for getting all the drinks. It really made the night.

> SETH
> It's just how I roll, Jules. No problems, no problems. You'll see.

Jules laughs and Seth sees that his charm is working.

> SETH (CONT'D)
> Uh. . . you know. . . I love talking, and conversing with you, you're so good at it, but I can't hear you. All this music. Could we just go on the. . . uh. . . balcony or something?

Jules eyes Seth suspiciously. Seth just looks at her, smiling drunkenly.

> JULES
> Um. . . why not? I haven't conversed in ages. Let's do it.

Screenplay

Superbad

Jules walks out of the kitchen. He finishes off his beer and then, happy as shit, drunkenly dances out of the kitchen and after Jules.

INT. JULES' BROTHER'S BEDROOM – CONTINUOUS

Evan practically holds Becca up, almost dropping her several times, as they stumble into Jules' bedroom. Becca puts down the tequila and starts kissing Evan, but it's not nice kissing, it's sloppy porno kissing with way too much tongue. After a few moments Evan pulls away and looks at the remarkably drunk Becca.

>   EVAN
> Are you okay?

>   BECCA
> I so flirt with you in Math.

>   EVAN
> Oh man. Becca. . . I want to tell you, I mean, I've wanted to tell you, for a long time—

>   BECCA
> I know. I've wanted to get with you so hard.

Becca kisses him.

>   BECCA (CONT'D)
> Like. . . so hard.

Becca yanks him onto the bed and starts sloppily kissing him again. Evan doesn't know what to do. She tries to take off Evan's shirt, but is way too inebriated to undo the buttons. Evan yanks it off.

>   BECCA (CONT'D)
> Good. . .

Becca stands up and starts to waver back and forth. She looks like she's about to tip over, but she catches herself and sloppily tries to strike a sexy pose like a model.

Evan watches in dread as she starts to strip, pulling her shirt over her head, completely failing to look sexual.

As Evan watches the tragedy unfold, he grabs the bottle of tequila and takes a big swig. Becca sits on the floor and concentrates on untying her shoes.

>   BECCA (CONT'D)
> What the fuck. . . stupid shoe. . .

Evan moves over to help her. He can't do it either.

>   EVAN
> Shit. Can you, like, slip out?

Becca tries to squeeze her feet out, but she can't. She grabs a pair of scissors off a desk.

>   EVAN (CONT'D)
> Whoa. Fuckin'. . . careful.

She snips off the knot and slips her shoe off.

>   BECCA
> You. . . take off your pants. . .
>   (drunkenly waving the scissors)
> Or I'll cut 'em off.

Becca laughs as she staggers to her feet and start kissing Evan. He starts taking off his pants.

>   EVAN
>   (nervous)
> I'm taking my pants off.

INT. JULES' STAIRCASE – MOMENTS LATER

Nicola leads Fogell up the stairs.

>   NICOLA
> I've never been with an older guy before.

>   FOGELL
> Well. . . it's way better.

EXT. JULES' HOUSE – SIDE OF THE HOUSE – CONTINUOUS

Jules and Seth step out onto the front porch. There is no one else out there. The moment the door closes behind them, Seth turns to Jules and puts his hands on her hips. He stares into her eyes and moves in for the kiss.

Jules instantly pulls back.

>   JULES
> Whoa! Whoa! Slow down.

>   SETH
> What? What's wrong?

JULES
I'd... uh... prefer if we did this at some other time.

SETH
(confused)
But... there is no other time. School's up! This is the only time... what's wrong with now?

JULES
Well, you're drunk. Like, really, really drunk.

SETH
So? So are you.

JULES
I'm not drunk at all. I don't even drink.

Seth is absolutely shocked.

SETH
You don't drink? But... but, you told me to get the liquor!

JULES
Yeah, I'm... uh... throwin' a party, remember?

SETH
You don't drink!?!

JULES
No. I don't drink.

SETH
And you, don't want to... uh, you know...

JULES
Uh, no. Not right now, thank you very much.

Seth looks at Jules and realizes that he's screwed up. His eyes start to water.

SETH
Ahhh....man...fuck....

Seth starts to cry.

JULES
Are you crying?

SETH
No! Yeah, so what if I am? I'm a fucking idiot and it was my last chance! So I should be crying.

JULES
Last chance to do what?

SETH
To make you my girlfriend for the summer, okay? There! You're, like, the coolest person that's ever talked to me, and I thought we'd both be drunk, but...

JULES
What would me being drunk have anything to do with it?

SETH
'Cause you'd never get with me sober! Look at me!
(beat)
And now look at you!

Seth starts sobbing even harder as Jules stares at him.

INT. JULES' BROTHER'S ROOM – CONTINUOUS

Evan sitting on the bed in only his boxers, and Becca is just getting her pants off, leaving her only in her lingerie. Evan's eyes widen. She looks at Evan and rubs her breasts in a very un-sexy way.

BECCA
I wore this for you. Here we go...

Becca crawls onto the bed, pushes Evan down, and starts seriously making out with him, drunker and sloppier than ever.

BECCA (CONT'D)
Evan, I'm so wet.

EVAN
(still nervous)
You look so beautiful.

Becca shoves her hand down Evan's boxers. Evan jolts, terrified!

BECCA
You've got such a smooth cock.

Screenplay

                    EVAN
          Um. . . thank you. I've thought you were a
          really incredible person for a really long time.

Evan looks really nervous as Becca's hand starts moving up and down.

                    BECCA
          You've got to get hard for me. . . real hard.

                    EVAN
          I'm. . . I'm..I'm about to. But first I just want to
          tell you exactly how I—

                    BECCA
          I'm gonna suck your dick so good.

Evan is taken aback.

                    EVAN
          You don't have to do that, you know, we can
          start this relationship on something more than
          just that.

                    BECCA
          Yeah, Evan. I know.
              (in a sultry, whispery voice)
          Evan, oh. . . I want you to finger fuck my pussy,
          then eat me hard.

                    EVAN
          Jesus Christ.

Evan sits up.

                    BECCA
          What's wrong?

Beat.

                    EVAN
          You don't want to do this.

                    BECCA
          Yeah I do, I want to fuck you. Just let it happen.

                    EVAN
          Look, you know I really like you, Becca, but this
          is. . . it's just too intense. And I'm so drunk I
          don't even know how to, like, process this. It
          doesn't feel right.

                    BECCA
          Oh man. You're just being a pussy.

                    EVAN
          What? Did you just call me a. . . pussy?

                    BECCA
          Yeah. . . a scared little pussy—

PUKE! Evan watches in horror as Becca vomits all over Jules' bed.

                    EVAN
          Oh god! Oh. . .

                    BECCA
          I need Gaby. . . Gaby. . .

                    EVAN
          I'll. . . uh. . . I'll go get her. Are you going to be
          okay?

                    BECCA
          Oh God, oh God, oh. . . I'm puking. . .

PUKE! Evan winces as she throws up again.

INT. JULES PARENTS'S BEDROOM – CONTINUOUS

Fogell is laying on his back on the bed and Nicola is straddling him. They are kissing. Nicola sits up and takes Fogell's hand and starts sucking his fingers.

                    FOGELL
              (matter-of-fact)
          I've got a boner.

                    NICOLA
          Good. Do you have a condom?

He pulls a condom out.

                    FOGELL
          And lube.

He pulls out a little bottle of lube.

EXT. JULES' HOUSE – SIDE OF THE HOUSE – NIGHT

Seth and Jules are both seated on the stairs. Seth has his face in his hands. Jules is patting him on the back, but clearly feels awkward.

JULES
Seth, you. . . uh. . .

Seth looks up at her, drunk as hell, his eyes half-open.

JULES (CONT'D)
You didn't blow it, you're a—

Seth blanks out and falls forward. BAM! He head-butts Jules in the face!

JULES (CONT'D)
AAAHHH!

Jules clutches her eye as Seth slumps onto the patio floor, unconscious. She gets up, yelling in pain, as Seth opens his eyes.

JULES (CONT'D)
Seth! What the fuck!

SETH
. . . help me. . .

Jules storms into the house, leaving Seth lying on the front porch. He wiggles around a bit.

SETH (CONT'D)
. . . sorry. . .

Seth passes out again. A few moments go by, when SUDDENLY a cop car pulls up in front of the house. Seth opens his eyes and sees the cops.

SETH (CONT'D)
Oh no.

Two cops get out and start harassing two kids smoking a joint on the front lawn. One of them turns on their flashlight and Seth sees – it's OFFICER SLATER and MICHAELS!!!

SETH (CONT'D)
. . . Evan. . .

INT. JULES' HOUSE – CONTINUOUS

Evan, sitting on the couch next to Miroki (Evan's partner from cooking class), drinking a bottle of tequila. He's absolutely smashed.

EVAN
Life's bullshit, huh, Miroki?

Evan passes out. Suddenly, Seth bursts into the room. He spots Evan, grabs his shirt, and tries to pull him to his feet.

SETH
Come on. Get up man!

Just then, Jesse (the guy who spat on Seth in the beginning) walks by.

JESSE
Hey! Have fun boning each other on grad night!

Jesse and his buddies laugh their asses off when, suddenly—

KNOCK! KNOCK! KNOCK! The loud authoritative knocking echoes through the party and everyone looks to the door, knowing it can only mean one thing. Someone opens the door, revealing Officer Slater and Officer Michaels! They talk to whoever answered the door, oblivious of Evan and Seth.

OFFICER SLATER
We had a complaint about the noise. It looks like you're having a nice little party here.

OFFICER MICHAELS
A nice little underage drinking party.

SETH
(to Evan)
We gotta go!

Seth shakes Evan to try to wake him. Nothing.

SETH (CONT'D)
Oh. . . man. C'mon. I'm trying to save you.

The cops scan the party and are pleased to see it is nothing more than a high school party.

Seth looks at the unconscious Evan, then to the approaching cops.

Screenplay

SETH (CONT'D)
Let's go, buddy.

Seth bends down and picks Evan up, holding him like a child in his arms. He starts making his way to the back-door.

INT. JULES' HOUSE – DANCING ROOM – NIGHT

Drunkenly, Seth moves into the adjoining room. As he stumbles onward he passes by a nearby coffee table and consequently runs Evan's head along it, knocking an array of beer bottles onto the ground.

SHIRLEY
What the fuck, Seth?

SETH
He's my best friend!

Seth drops Evan.

SETH (CONT'D)
Oh no!

Looks back toward the living room and sees the cops there. He manically tries to pick up Evan, but is so drunk he can't seem to do it.

INT. JULES' HOUSE – LIVING ROOM – NIGHT

ANGLE ON: SLATER AND MICHAELS

The cops walk forwards into the house, ushering people out.

OFFICER SLATER
Okay, everyone out. Party's over. Get out of here!

OFFICER MICHAELS
Move it! Leave all your beer and alcohol behind!

Michaels heads towards the back of the house.

INT. JULES' HOUSE – DANCING ROOM – NIGHT

Seth, using all his drunken might, lifts Evan up once more. He glances back and sees Officer Michaels approaching!

He looks forward at the sea of people between him and the back door. With Evan in his arms, he starts aggressively pushing through the crowd.

PARTY GOER #2
Hey! Watch where you're fucking going!

SETH
Shut up!

Michaels makes his way into the same room.

OFFICER MICHAELS
Everyone in this room, get out of this house, now!

Officer Michaels sees the back door open. He sees the back of Seth's head as he carries Evan out and thinks nothing of it.

EXT. JULES' BACKYARD – CONTINUOUS

Seth carries Evan across the back yard. Seth stumbles and falls, dropping Evan once again. He quickly scoops him up and carries him to the woods behind Jules' house. We see Jules, standing by the window with a bag of frozen peas on her eye. She is very confused when she sees Seth carrying Evan into the night.

Seth, exhausted, marches forward.

INT. JULES PARENTS'S BEDROOM – CONTINUOUS

Fogell is on top of Nicola in the missionary position.

NICOLA
Oh. . . uh. . . oh. . .

FOGELL
It's. . . it's in.
(beat)
It's in.

Fogell wears the greatest look of accomplishment one could possibly imagine.

SUDDENLY, Officer Slater bursts into the room and flicks on the lights.

FOGELL (CONT'D)
What the hell?

Nicola screams, grabs her clothes, and runs into the bathroom.

OFFICER SLATER
McLovin? What the fuck?

Superbad

                    FOGELL
Officer Slater?

                    OFFICER SLATER
You ran away from us!
        (turns to the door)
Michaels! Get up here!

                    FOGELL
No! I hit my head when we crashed. I was all
disoriented and I just wandered off, confused.
Seriously!

Officer Michaels appears in the doorway.

                    OFFICER MICHAELS
McLovin! What the fuck?

Slater take Fogell's arms and handcuffs him.

                    FOGELL
What? No! No!

Nicola, now dressed, emerges from the bathroom. She screams and runs out.

                    OFFICER MICHAELS
McLovin. . . were you getting laid?

                    FOGELL
No! Yes. . . look!, I'm not really even—

Fogell stands up.

                    OFFICER SLATER
Hey! Sit your ass down and keep it down.

Michaels looks at the angered Slater.

                    OFFICER MICHAELS
        (to Slater)
Hey man, come here for one sec.

They step aside and whisper so Fogell can't hear.

                    OFFICER MICHAELS (CONT'D)
You just cock-blocked McLovin?

                    OFFICER SLATER
        (a little sheepish)
What. . . well, yeah, but he. . . I didn't realize. . .

                    OFFICER MICHAELS
Slater, what the fuck is wrong with you, man?
When did we start cock-blocking? We should be
guiding his cock, not blocking it.

ANGLE ON: Fogell

Terrified beyond belief, he watches the cops continue to whisper to one another.

                    FOGELL
Listen, guys, seriously, I'm not who you think, I
swear to god! Please, just listen to me. . . I can't
go to jail. . .

The officer's stare Fogell down.

Beat.

The two cops burst out laughing hysterically.

                    OFFICER SLATER
        (laughing his ass off)
Yeah!! You're going to fuckin' Azkaban!!!

                    FOGELL
What?

                    OFFICER MICHAELS
You are the funniest fuckin' kid I have ever met!

                    OFFICER SLATER
We've been fuckin' with you! Jesus! I love this
kid!

                    FOGELL
I don't understand!

                    OFFICER SLATER
We know you're not twenty five! What are we,
morons? My god! What are you? Sixteen?

                    FOGELL
Seventeen.

                    OFFICER MICHAELS
Seventeen! Ha! We had you going, McLovin!

                    FOGELL
So. . . I'm not going to jail.

OFFICER SLATER
No. We cock-blocked. We owe you a good time.
You're coming to hang out with us.

Fogell thinks.

FOGELL
Wait. Could you guys do me a huge favor?

EXT. JULES' FRONT YARD - CONTINUOUS

All the kids from the party have congregated in the front yard. The cop car is parked right in front. We see the Officers, carrying bags of confiscated booze, dragging the handcuffed Fogell through the crowd of kids. Fogell is struggling a good deal.

OFFICER SLATER
This kid's fucking crazy.

FOGELL
Let go of me you piece of shit cops! I'll fucking kill your asses, you understand me? Kill 'em!

OFFICER MICHAELS
I can't hold him! He has the strength of ten men!

ANGLE ON: A GROUP OF KIDS, INCLUDING JESSE.

PARTY GOER #3
Holy shit, is Fogell a bad ass or what.

JESSE
Yeah! Stupid pigs.

SUDDENLY, a WAD OF SPIT hits Slater in the shoulder! He turns and sees Jesse, the guy who spat on Seth. Slater walks over and bashes the kid in the face with his nightstick. The kid drops. They throw Fogell into the back of the cop car.

INT. COP CAR - CONTINUOUS

The cops both get in and slam their doors.

OFFICER SLATER
Man, that is gonna get you so much ass.

OFFICER MICHAELS
Slater. I think I know what to do about the car.

EXT. STREET - CONTINUOUS

Drunk, joyful, and out of breath and still carrying Evan in his arms, Seth stops running. Evan's eyes open.

EVAN
Are. . . are you carrying me?

SETH
No! I'm saving you! From the cops.

EVAN
You saved me?

Evan drunkenly tries to understand what Seth is talking about.

EVAN (CONT'D)
I don't really know what you're talking about,
but thank you, man.
(beat)
Should I walk now?

SETH
Yeah. If you want.

Seth puts Evan down. They start walking side by side and continue on for a lengthy beat as Evan slowly regains his composure.

EVAN
Shit.
(beat)
Wanna sleep at my house, man? You're my best friend!

SETH
Yeah! Sleepover! Fuckin. . . you got pizza bagels still?

EVAN
Yeah!!!!

SETH
Nice!

Superbad

INT. COP CAR – DRIVING – LATER THAT NIGHT

As Slater drives through a red light, Michaels hands Fogell a piece of paper and a pen.

> OFFICER MICHAELS
> . . . and by signing this you are officially saying that as we stopped you from being mugged, a crack-head stole our cruiser and did God knows what with it. You're cool to sign it?

> FOGELL
> Of course. I owe you my life.

> OFFICER MICHAELS
> Thanks to. . . what was your name again?

> FOGELL
> Fogell.

> OFFICER SLATER
> Ah. . . we're calling you McLovin.

> OFFICER MICHAELS
> We might actually get off probation.

> FOGELL
> So. . . um, what did you guys do?
> (back-pedalling)
> I mean, you don't have to tell me.

> OFFICER MICHAELS
> Well. . . we trashed two other cars. The first time wasn't our fault, and the second time a bee flew in and Slater crashed the car.

> OFFICER SLATER
> To cover, he relieved himself in the cruiser and told the captain that a bum threw a bottle of piss at us. Michaels saved my ass on that one.

EXT. ABANDONED-LOOKING PARKING LOT – CONTINUOUS

The cop car drives into the empty parking lot and starts spinning donuts. It stops. Fogell and Officer Michaels get out, both smiling. The driver side window rolls down, reveal Slater.

> OFFICER SLATER
> Now what I'm about to show you is pretty much the greatest move in donut-spinning history. Behold: the reverse figure-eight.

Slater drives to the other side of the lot.

> FOGELL
> So, like, what's your official position on Nicola?

> OFFICER MICHAELS
> If you were in, you were in. You are no longer a virgin, end of story. Screw cumming.

Suddenly, Slater guns it and speeds across the lot, slamming the breaks, spinning wildly in several erratic backward donuts.

Slater completely loses control of the car. He smashes through a bunch of shopping carts and slams into a light post, completely fucking up the cruiser.

Slater tries to open his door, but it won't budge. He crawls out the missing windshield, slumping onto the ground. Sparks shower down from the lights above.

> OFFICER SLATER
> Alright. Fuckin' crazy. Let's do this thing.

EXT. ABANDONED-LOOKING PARKING LOT – MOMENTS LATER

Fogell and Slater stand back as Michaels walks towards the cruiser with a flaming Molotov cocktail in his hand.

> OFFICER SLATER
> Don't blow yourself up, dumb ass!

Michaels hurls the cocktail at the cruiser; it bursts into flames.

> FOGELL
> Can we shoot at it?

> OFFICER SLATER
> I don't know, can you?

Slater hands Fogell his gun. With a huge smile, Fogell raises the gun sideways gangsta style, aims it at the police cruiser, and BLASTS off round after round.

Screenplay

INT. EVAN'S BASEMENT – NIGHT

Seth and Evan are lying in sleeping bags beside one another. They are laughing very hard, still drunk off their asses.

          SETH
I can't believe she said that shit.

          EVAN
Oh my lord. You have no idea!

They laugh harder.

          EVAN (CONT'D)
And then you saved me, man! I fucking love you!

          SETH
I fucking love you, too, man! I'm not embarrassed, I just love you!

          EVAN
Why don't we say that more? It feels good! I love you more than my brother, man. Like, when you went away for Easter last year, I, like, missed you. You know?

          SETH
I missed you, too. Come here, man.

Seth grabs Evan and they hug.

          SETH (CONT'D)
We'll always be friends. 'Cause we love each other.

They stop hugging and sit back down. Their laughter slows down and there is a moment of silence.

          SETH (CONT'D)
Like, three weeks ago I was in your room and, like, you were taking a dump and. . . I saw your residence placement thingy. I totally saw you're living with Fogell. So, like—

          EVAN
I'm sorry, man.

          SETH
Don't be! Don't be! *I'm* sorry. I was being a bitch.

          EVAN
I need you to know that it's not like I even want to live with Fogell; it's just that I'm really afraid of living with strangers.

There is a moment of silence.

          SETH
You know. . . I was pissed off I didn't get with Jules, but, like. . . we really got through a lot of our shit, you know?

          EVAN
Yeah, me too. Like, yeah. . . at least we kind of came together, again.

Beat.

          EVAN (CONT'D)
Good night, Seth. I love you.

          SETH
Night, Evan. Love you, man.

INT. EVAN'S HOUSE – BASEMENT – THE NEXT MORNING

Evan wakes up and looks over at Seth, who is also waking. They look at each other extremely awkwardly, almost as though they drunkenly had sex with each other last night.

          EVAN
Oh. . . uh. . . hey. Morning.

          SETH
Uh. . . morning.

They stare at each other, uncomfortable.

          EVAN
You sleep good?

          SETH
Yeah. This is a really good pillow. Ergonomic.

          EVAN
Um. . .

Seth looks at his watch.

          SETH
Maybe I should get going.

Superbad

Screenplay

                    EVAN
          You don't have to. I'm not, like, doing anything.

Beat.

                    SETH
          Oh. . . do you want to hang out? I was. . . gonna
          go to the mall, actually.

                    EVAN
          Oh. Cool, well, can I come? I need a comforter.
          For college.

                    SETH
          Yeah. That'd be nice. I'd really like that.

INT. DEPARTMENT STORE – NEXT DAY

Evan is standing in the pants section of a department store. Seth walks out of the dressing room wearing jeans that are way too small.

                    EVAN
          Don't ask me. I don't give a shit if your pants
          look good.

                    SETH
          Well, I need someone's opinion.

                    EVAN
          Fine. They're way too small.

                    SETH
          Yeah, but when I was wearing your dad's pants
          last night I realized that if I buy pants that are
          too small it'll encourage me to lose weight. And
          in tight pants chicks'll kind of see the outline of
          my dick a little.

                    EVAN
          Yeah, the male camel toe look is really big this
          year.

Seth goes back into the dressing room and wriggles out of the pants. He walks out.

                    SETH
          These pants suck. Let's the get the fuck out of
          here.

INT. MALL – MOMENTS LATER

They walk through the mall, when suddenly, Evan sees Becca and Jules coming towards them.

ANGLE ON: Becca and Jules

                    BECCA
          Again, I'm so sorry. I can't believe I actually did
          that.

                    JULES
          I feel sorry that I'm making you buy me a new
          one.

                    BECCA
          I have to. It's puke.

ANGLE ON: Seth and Evan, frozen, no place to hide.

                    EVAN
          Holy shit!

Becca looks like hell and Jules has a horrible black eye.

                    SETH
          Is that them?

They stare at the two girls from afar.

                    EVAN
          Should we hide?

Becca looks and notices them. She waves and points them out to Jules. Seth and Evan wave back. The girls get up and start to walk over.

                    SETH
               (pretending to smile)
          Fuck that, man. I can't talk to her, look what I
          did to her!

                    EVAN
               (pretending to smile)
          Becca called me a pussy to my face! What am I
          going to say to her?

The girls walk up to them.

          BECCA   JULES
     Hi Evan, Seth.   Hey guys.

Superbad

    EVAN   SETH
 Hi Becca, Hi Jules.   Jules. Becca. Hi.

Everyone looks very embarrassed.

    SETH
Oh my god. I'm so sorry, Jules.

    JULES
It's okay.

    EVAN
 (to Becca)
How are you feeling?

    BECCA
Not bad, but not great, how about you?

    SETH
 (to Jules)
That looks terrible. No! I mean, it doesn't look terrible, it looks—

    JULES
Don't worry about it, Seth. It was an accident.

    EVAN
 (to Becca)
Did you have fun last night?

    JULES
 (to Seth)
Do you remember much?

    BECCA
 (to Evan)
I really don't remember much.

    SETH
 (to Jules)
Not really. I remember looking up, and you screaming at me. I don't remember crying.

    EVAN
I really don't remember anything.

Jules laughs.

    BECCA
 (to Evan)
I didn't puke on you, did I?

Evan laughs.

    EVAN
No, I dodged it. Whizzed right by me.

    SETH
 (to Jules)
But seriously, I acted like a fuckin' idiot last night. I'm really sorry, you didn't deserve that.

    BECCA
 (to Evan)
Yeah, I. . . um. . . I'm sorry, about all that. Thanks for being such a gentleman.

There is a moment of silence.

    SETH
You look good with a black eye.

They all chuckle a little.

    JULES
Thanks, smart guy. That's why I'm here. I have to get a shitload of cover-up for the grad photo.

    SETH
 (mortified)
Oh man. . .

    BECCA
Yeah, and I'm going to buy Jules a new comforter.

    EVAN
Oh! I have to get a comforter too, for college.

    JULES
 (flirtatiously, joking)
So, you gonna come buy me my cover-up, or what?

    SETH
Yes! Definitely. I'd love to. I had such bad acne last year, I became an expert on the stuff.

Screenplay

EVAN
You could get your college pants there.

SETH
Yeah, but wait. . . you drove me here, Evan drove me here, how do we—

JULES
I've got my dad's car. I'll take you home, and Evan can give Becca a lift.

BECCA
That sounds good.

EVAN
Maybe we can go eat after?

BECCA
Sweet.

Seth and Evan look at each other, odd smiles on both their faces. They didn't blow it.

SETH
So, uh, I'll call you later.

EVAN
Yeah man, you have my number.

JULES
Come on, Seth. Let's go.

Jules pulls Seth towards the escalator. Evan and Becca start walking in the opposite direction.

As Seth descends the escalator, he looks back up at Evan, who looks back, too. They walk away from one another, Seth and Evan look back and give each other a small and yet emotionally-charged wave. A SLOW, GUT WRENCHING SOUL SONG STARTS TO PLAY. They look as though they're never going to see each other again.

As Jules and Seth walk into a department store and Becca and Evan walk the other way, the music swells to a mind-fuckingly awesome crescendo, and we humbly fade to black. . .

THE END

END CREDIT SEQUENCE:

We flip through Seth's seemingly endless penis drawings from childhood. They are hilarious.

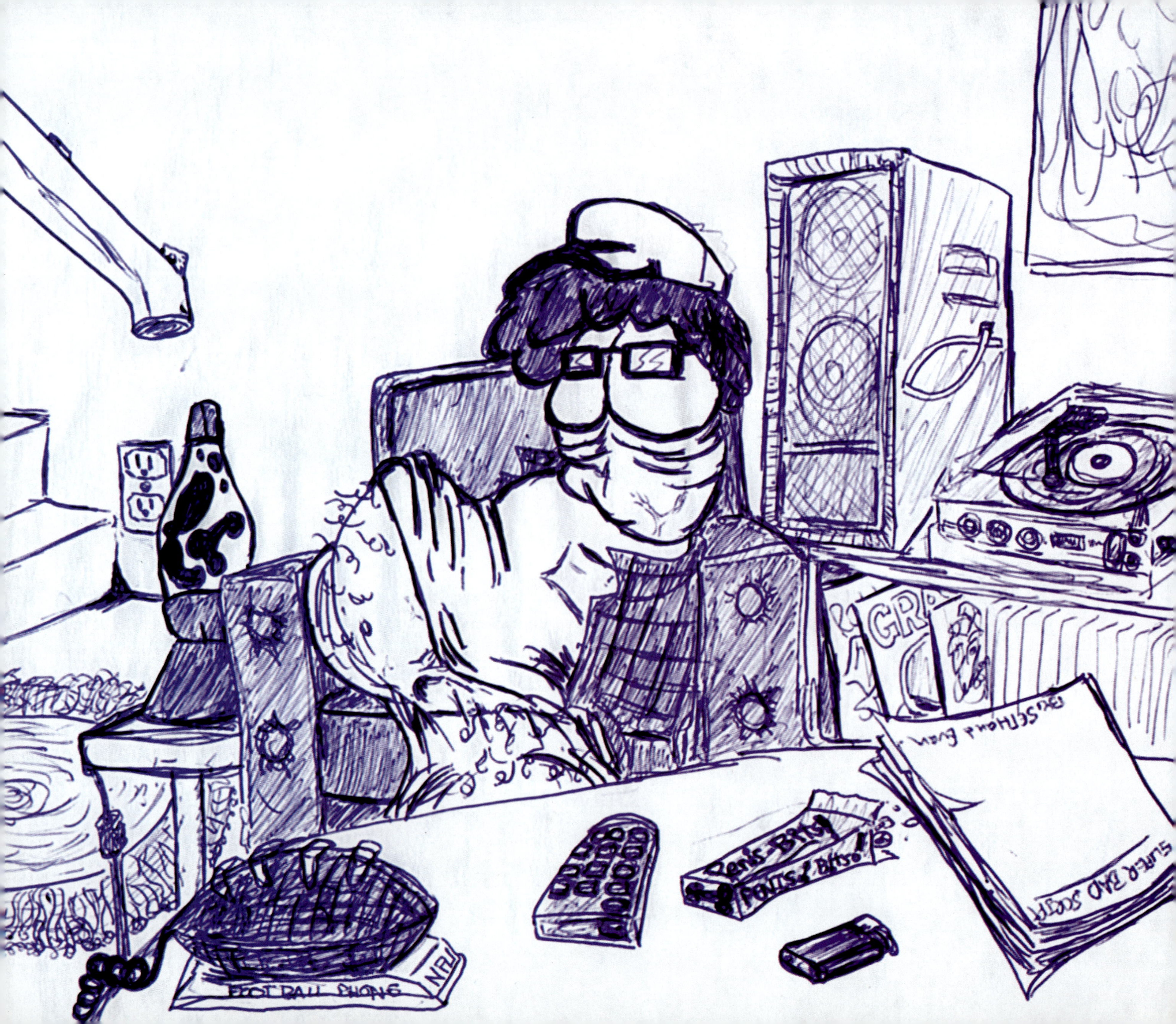
FOOTBALL PHONE
NFL
Penis Bits
PENIS & Bits!
SUPER BAD SCRIPT

credits

COLUMBIA PICTURES PRESENTS

AN APATOW COMPANY PRODUCTION

SUPERBAD

Jonah Hill

Michael Cera

Seth Rogen

Bill Hader

Kevin Corrigan

Joe Lo Truglio

Martha MacIsaac

Emma Stone

AND INTRODUCING

Christopher Mintz-Plasse

CASTING BY
Allison Jones

COSTUME DESIGNER
Debra McGuire

CO-PRODUCER
Dara Weintraub

MUSIC SUPERVISION BY
Jonathan Karp

MUSIC BY
Lyle Workman

EDITED BY
William Kerr

PRODUCTION DESIGNER
Chris Spellman

DIRECTOR OF PHOTOGRAPHY
Russ Alsobrook, ASC

EXECUTIVE PRODUCERS
Seth Rogen
Evan Goldberg

PRODUCED BY
Judd Apatow
Shauna Robertson

WRITTEN BY
Seth Rogen & Evan Goldberg

DIRECTED BY
Greg Mottola

CAST

Seth	Jonah Hill
Evan	Michael Cera
Fogell	Christopher Mintz-Plasse
Officer Slater	Bill Hader
Officer Michaels	Seth Rogen
Becca	Martha MacIsaac
Jules	Emma Stone
Nicola	Aviva
Francis the Driver	Joe Lo Truglio
Mark	Kevin Corrigan
Homeless Guy	Clement E. Blake
Liquor Store Cashier	Erica Vittina Phillips
Liquor Store Clerk	Joseph A. Nunez
Greg the Soccer Player	Dave Franco
Gaby	Marcella Lentz-Pope
Jesse	Scottie Gerbacia
Shirley	Laura Seay
Miroki	Roger Iwami
Prosthetic Leg Kid	Clint Mabry
Evan's Mom	Stacy Edwards
Father with Bat	Mark Rogen
Good Shopper Cashier	Charlie Hartsock
Old Lady	Dona Hardy
Good Shopper Security	Charley Rossman
Period Blood Girl	Carla Gallo
Quince Danbury	Ben Best

Superbad

Tut Long John Silver	Jody Hill
Patrick Manchester	Kevin Breznahan
Benji Austin	David Krumholtz
Billy Baybridge	Mousa Kraish
Coffee Fairmount	Nicholas Jasenovec
James Masselin	Martin Starr
Wild Bill Cherry	Keith Joseph Loneker
Kane Cloverdale	Matthew McKane
Scarlett Brighton	Lauren Miller
Tiger Greendragon	Peter Salett
Muffin Selby	Rakefet Abergel
Mrs. Hayworth	Brooke Dillman
Gym Teacher	Michael Naughton
Math Teacher	Steve Bannos
Young Seth	Casey Margolis
Young Becca	Laura Marano
Vagtastic Voyager	Matthew Bass
Vagtastic Voyage Girls	Aurora Snow
	Jenna Haze
Bartender	Ted Haigh
Bus Driver	Michael Fennessey
Elementary Principal	Brian Huskey
Party Teenagers	Clark Duke
	Stephen Borrello IV
	Naathan Phan
Teacher	Pamella D'Pella

Stunt Coordinator	Tim Trella
Stunts	Kenny Alexander
	Cody Gill
	Buddy Joe Hooker
	Mic Rodgers
	Michael Runyard
	Todd Warren
Unit Production Manager	Dara Weintraub
First Assistant Director	Scott Robertson
Second Assistant Director	Steven F. Beaupre
Production Supervisor	Christa Vausbinder
Art Director	Gerald Sullivan
Set Decorator	Robert Kensinger
Property Master	Michelle Spears
Script Supervisor	Ronit Ravich-Boss
Camera Operator	Steven H. Smith
First Assistant Camera	Jason Garcia
Second Assistant Camera	Rigney Sackley
"B" Camera Operator/Steadicam	Jerome Fauci
First Assistant "B" Camera	Timothy Kane
Second Assistant "B" Camera	Betty Chow

credits

Digital Imaging Technician . . Nick Theodorakis	Production Mixer . . . . Harrison D. Marsh	Set Designers . . . . Alicia Maccarone
	Boom Operator . . . . Tom Fox	Natalie Richards
Costume Supervisor . . . . . . Mary E. Walbridge	Video Assist . . . . Jay Huntoon	Leadman . . . . Thierry Labbe
Key Costumer . . . . Michael A. Russell	Video Playback . . . . Rick Whitfield	Graphic Designer . . . . Ted Haigh
Costumers . . . . Jennifer Iizuka	Special Effects Coordinator . . . . . . Bob Stoker	Storyboard Artist . . . . Darryl Henley
Edward Nino	Special Effects Technician . . . . . . Paul E. Vigil	Art Department Coordinator . . . . . Kat Wilson
Margaret Rogers		On-Set Dresser . . . . Mark Brooks
	Location Manager . . . . Christine Bonnem	Assistant Property Master . . . . . Kim Richey
Department Head Makeup . . . Kimberly Greene	Assistant Location Managers . . Jeffrey Garrett	Assistant Props . . . . Jeffrey Barnett
Key Makeup Artist . . . . Lana Horochowski	Matthew Messina	
Makeup Artist . . . . Maggie Fung	Christi Neubeiser	Construction Coordinator . . Karen D. Higgins
Special Makeup Effects by . . . . . . Robert Hall	Production Coordinator . . . . Sara Scarritt	General Foreman . . . . Steven Kissick
	Assistant Production	Labor Foreman . . . . Edward A. Giron
Department Head Hair . . . . Melissa A. Yonkey	Coordinators . . . . Carrie Arnold	Paint Supervisor . . . . Michael R. Blaich
Key Hair Stylist . . . . . Merribelle A. Anderson	Jenifer Bonisteel	Standby Painter . . . . Joey Genitempo
Hair Stylist . . . . Dena Fayne	Production Secretary . . . . Justin Giugno	Key Greens . . . . Jason Vanover
	Production Accountant . . . . Edward Allen	
Chief Lighting	Assistant Accountants . . . . Beth Waller	Unit Publicist . . . . Kym Langlie
Technician . . . . . . Christopher Napolitano	Saundra Marie Ardito	Still Photographer . . . . Melissa Moseley
Assistant Chief Lighting		2nd Second Assistant Director . . Nicole Swasey
Technician . . . . Ron Alexus		
Rigging Gaffer . . . . Dave Parks		Assistants to Mr. Mottola . . . . Elisabeth Stone
		John Schwert
Key Grip . . . . T. Daniel Scaringi		Assistants to Mr. Apatow . . . Andrew Epstein
Best Boy Grip . . . . Robert Chinello		Greg Cohen
Dolly Grips . . . . Paul E. Sutton		Lisa Yadavaia
Michael Wahl		
Rigging Key Grip . . . . Robert J. Reilly		

137

Superbad

Assistants to Ms. Robertson	....	Paul Sweeny
		Chelsey Dailey
Assistant to Mr. Rogen & Mr. Goldberg	....	Matthew Bass
Assistant to Ms. Weintraub	....	Tora Chung
Production Assistants	....	Sage Asteak
		Cris DeArce
		Scott Koche
		Mikki Levi
		Allan Marasco
		Gunnar Moulton
		Brad Pero
		Stephen Richards
		Hirotatsu Taniguchi
		Derek Wade
Casting Associate	....	Dorian Frankel
Extras Casting	....	Central Casting
Catering by	....	Gala Catering
Craft Service	....	Chance P. Tassone
		Joseph Milito
Studio Teacher	....	Nancy A. Flint
Medic	....	Ericka Bryce Poniewaz
Transportation Captain	.....	Mike Menapace
Transportation Co-Captain		James D. D'Amico

POST PRODUCTION

Additional Editor	....	Michael L. Sale
1st Assistant Editor	....	Dov Samuel
Assistant Editors	....	Laura Yanovich
		Kristen Young
		Stacey Clipp
Apprentice Editor	....	Brian Scott Olds
Supervising Sound Editor	...	George Anderson
Assistant Sound Editors	......	Cherie Tamai
		Ann Ducommun
Dialogue Editors	....	James Matheny
		Larry Kemp
Sound Effects Editor	....	Cindy Marty
Supervising ADR Editor	....	Tammy Fearing
Foley Editor	....	Joe Schiff
Foley Artists	....	Pamela Nedd Kahn
		Vincent Guisetti
Foley Mixer	....	Kyle Rochlin
Supervising Sound Mixers	....	Marc Fishman
		Tony Lamberti
Loop Group	....	The Reel Team

Post Sound Services Provided by .... Sony Pictures Studios, Culver City, California

Music Editor	....	Jonathan Karp
Score Mixer	....	Chris Fogel
Music Contractor	....	Gina Zimmitti
Music Prep	....	JoAnn Kane

Bootsy Collins & The Superbad Band

Bootsy Collins — bass, vocals
Bernie Worrell — clavinet, organ
Clyde Stubblefield — drums
John "Jab'o" Sparks — drums
Phelps "Catfish" Collins — guitar
Luis Conte — percussion
Jeff Babko — organ, clavinet, moog
Lyle Workman — guitar
Jerry Hey — trumpet, orchestrator

CHE D'ick

credits

Main Title Design by............Yard VFX

End Titles by......Right Lobe Design Group

Digital Intermediate by....Technicolor Digital Intermediates

Digital Colorist...........John Persichetti

Negative Cutter..............Mo Henry

Visual Effects by............Pacific Vision
Pacific Title

Filmed at Sony Pictures Studios
Culver City, California

MUSIC

"Too Hot To Stop"
Written by Fred Freeman and Harry L. Nehls
Performed by The Bar-Kays
Courtesy of The Island Def Jam Music Group
Under license from Universal Music Enterprises

"Soul Finger"
Written by James Alexander,
Ronnie Caldwell, Ben Cauley,
Carl Cunningham, Phalon R. Jones, Jr.
and Jimmy King
Performed by The Bar-Kays
Courtesy of Atlantic Recording Corp.
By arrangement with Warner Music Group
Film & TV Licensing

"Do Me"
Written by Kenneth Gamble and Leon Huff
Performed by Jean Knight
Courtesy of Stax Records
By arrangement with Concord Music Group, Inc.

"Roda"
Written by João Augusto and Gilberto Gil
Performed by Sergio Mendes & Brasil '66
Courtesy of A&M Records
Under license from Universal Music Enterprises

"Bustin' Out (On Funk)"
Written and Performed by Rick James
Courtesy of Motown Records
Under license from Universal Music Enterprises

"Are You Man Enough"
Written by Dennis Lambert and Brian Potter
Performed by The Four Tops
Courtesy of Geffen Records
Under license from Universal Music Enterprises

"High Class"
Written by Brian Lapin, Terence Yoshiaki
Graves and Michael Fratantuno
Performed by The Transcenders
Courtesy of Transcenders, LLC

"Why Do I Cry?"
Written by Barry Tashian
Performed by The Remains
Courtesy of Epic Records
By arrangement with SONY BMG
MUSIC ENTERTAINMENT

"Stranglehold"
Written and Performed by Ted Nugent
Courtesy of Epic Records
By arrangement with SONY BMG MUSIC ENTERTAINMENT

"This Is Your Captain"
Written by Ian Blurton
Performed by C'mon
Courtesy of Maple Music
By arrangement with Coda Music

"Echoes"
Written and Performed by The Rapture
Courtesy of Mercury Records Limited
Under license from Universal Music Enterprises

139

Superbad

"Big Poppa"
Written by Notorious B.I.G., Ronald Isley,
Rudolph Isley, O'Kelly Isley, Ernie Isley, Marvin
Isley and Chris Jasper
Performed by Notorious B.I.G.
Courtesy of Bad Boy Records LLC
By arrangement with Warner Music Group Film
& TV Licensing
Contains a sample of "Between The Sheets"
Performed by The Isley Brothers
Courtesy of Epic Records
By arrangement with SONY BMG
MUSIC ENTERTAINMENT

"Shake"
Written by Joey Levine and Kris Resnick
Performed by The Friggs
Courtesy of Apex Recording Service
By arrangement with Bug

"Dangerous Woman (With A 45 In Her Hand)"
Written by Robert Ellen
Performed by Sonny Terry & Brownie McGhee
Courtesy of Mainstream Records Inc.

"Policy Game"
Written by Robert Ellen
Performed by Lightnin' Hopkins
Courtesy of Mainstream Records Inc.

"Chop Chop You're Dead"
Written by Zack Frank, Simon Toye,
Matt Winters and Craig Nordemann
Performed by Cities In Dust
Courtesy of Paper Bag Records
By arrangement with Coda Music

"Journey To The Center Of Your Mind"
Written by Ted Nugent and Steven O. Farmer
Performed by Ted Nugent & The Amboy Dukes
Courtesy of Mainstream Records Inc.

"These Eyes"
Written by Burton Cummings
and Randy Bachman

"Ace Of Spades"
Written by Ian Kilminster, Edward Clarke
and Philip Taylor
Performed by Motörhead
Courtesy of Sanctuary Records

"Baby Please Don't Go"
Written by Robert Ellen
Performed by Ted Nugent & The Amboy Dukes
Courtesy of Mainstream Records Inc.

"These Eyes"
Written by Burton Cummings
and Randy Bachman
Performed by The Guess Who
Courtesy of The RCA Records Label
By arrangement with SONY BMG
MUSIC ENTERTAINMENT

"Here I Come"
Written by Karl Jenkins, Richard Nichols,
Malik Smart, Ahmir Thompson
and Tarik Trotter
Performed by The Roots featuring
Malik B. & Dice Raw
Courtesy of The Island Def Jam Music Group
Under license from Universal Music
Enterprises

"I'm Your Boogie Man"
Written by Harry Wayne Casey
and Richard Finch
Performed by KC & The Sunshine Band
Courtesy of Rhino Entertainment Company
By arrangement with Warner Music Group
Film & TV Licensing

"Blow Your Whistle"
Written by Yung Berg, Patrick Batiste,
Jules Batiste and William Warner
Performed by Morgan Smith
Courtesy of Interscope Records
Under license from Universal Music Enterprises

140

"My Favorite Mutiny"
Written by Tarik Collins, Talib Kweli
and Boots Riley
Performed by The Coup
Courtesy of Epitaph

"My Lady"
Written by Jeremy Ball and M. Sagapolutele
Performed by Mareko
Courtesy of Dawn Raid Entertainment

"Capital S.A."
Written by Nathan Holmes, Daniel Taupe
Maoate and Demetrius Christian Savelio
Performed by Alphrisk featuring Savage
Courtesy of Dawn Raid Entertainment

"Pork And Beef"
Written by Boots Riley
Performed by The Coup
Courtesy of Epitaph

"Panama"
Written by David Lee Roth, Alex
Van Halen and Edward Van Halen
Performed by Van Halen
Courtesy of Warner Bros. Records Inc.
By arrangement with Warner Music Group
Film & TV Licensing

"P.S. I Love You"
Written and Performed by Curtis Mayfield
Courtesy of Rhino Entertainment Company/
Curtom Classics, Inc.
By arrangement with Warner Music Group
Film & TV Licensing

© 2007 Columbia Pictures Industries, Inc.
All Rights Reserved

Columbia Pictures Industries, Inc., is the author of
this film for the purpose of copyright and other laws.

Seth's Drawings by David Goldberg

Ultimate Fighting Championship® footage provided
by Zuffa, LLC © 2005. All Rights Reserved.

This is a work of fiction. The characters, incidents, and locations portrayed and the names herein are fictitious, and any similarity to or identification with the location, name, character or history of any person, product or entity is entirely coincidental and unintentional.

This motion picture photoplay is protected pursuant to the provisions of the laws of the United States of America and other countries. Any unauthorized duplication and/or distribution of this photoplay may result in civil liability and criminal prosecution.

APATOW PRODUCTIONS

COLUMBIA PICTURES

A Columbia Pictures Release

A SONY PICTURES ENTERTAINMENT COMPANY

The Filmmakers

SETH ROGEN & EVAN GOLDBERG (Screenwriters, Executive Producers) grew up in Vancouver, British Columbia, together and wrote their first screenplay, *Superbad*, when they were 13 years old.

After moving to Los Angeles, Rogen served as a staff writer on Judd Apatow's television series *Undeclared*. The duo went on to write for Sacha Baron Cohen's cult hit *Da Ali G Show*, as well as the feature film *Pineapple Express*, which the pair also executive produced. In addition, Rogen co-wrote the upcoming Owen Wilson comedy *Drillbit Taylor*, directed by Steven Brill.

Rogen served as co-producer on Apatow's sleeper hit *The 40-Year-Old-Virgin*, and executive produced, along with Goldberg, Apatow's blockbuster hit *Knocked Up*, starring Rogen, Katherine Heigl, Leslie Mann, and Paul Rudd.

Rogen's first major acting role was in Judd Apatow's critically acclaimed comedy *Freaks and Geeks*. When that show ended, Apatow invited Rogen to become part of his new show, *Undeclared*, as both a writer and an actor. Rogen's other acting credits include *You, Me and Dupree*; *Donny Darko*; *Anchorman: The Legend of Ron Burgundy*; *The 40-Year-Old Virgin*; and, of course, as Officer Michaels in *Superbad*.

Rogen will have voice roles in the upcoming *Kung Fu Panda*, *Horton Hears a Who*, and *The Spiderwick Chronicles*.

Seth Rogen and Evan Goldberg are currently writing *The Green Hornet*, which will star Rogen.

GREG MOTTOLA (Director) is the writer and director of the movie *The Daytrippers* (1997), starring Hope Davis, Parker Posey, Liev Schreiber, Anne Meara, Campbell Scott, and Stanley Tucci. *The Daytrippers* was chosen for the Cannes Film Festival and Toronto International Film Festival, and it was awarded the audience and jury prizes at the Deauville Festival of American Films. Mottola went on to team with Judd Apatow and Seth Rogen as the director of several episodes of the Fox television series *Undeclared*. He has also directed episodes of *Arrested Development* and HBO's *The Comeback*.

Greg attended graduate film school at Columbia University, where he studied with Sidney Lumet, David Mamet, and George Roy Hill. He has also acted—not particularly well, he says—in the Woody Allen movies *Celebrity* and *Hollywood Ending*. Mottola hopes some day to have a better bio.

JUDD APATOW (Producer) made his feature directorial debut with the 2005 summer box-office smash *The 40-Year-Old Virgin* starring Steve Carell. He followed up with the blockbuster comedy *Knocked Up*, starring Katherine Heigl, Seth Rogen, Leslie Mann and Paul Rudd; Apatow also wrote and produced the film, which has gone on to take in over $140 million at the U.S. box office. Apatow has several films slated for release from Columbia Pictures, including *Walk Hard—The Dewey Cox Story*, which Apatow is co-writing with director Jake Kasdan and producing; *Pineapple

The Filmmakers

Express, produced by Apatow and for which he teamed on the story with screenwriters Seth Rogen & Evan Goldberg; *Step Brothers*, which he is producing, starring Will Ferrell and John C. Reilly; and *You Don't Mess with the Zohan*, which Apatow co-wrote with Adam Sandler and Robert Smigel. He is also producing *Drillbit Taylor* and *Forgetting Sarah Marshall*, both set for release next spring.

Apatow also produced *Talladega Nights: The Ballad of Ricky Bobby*, starring Will Ferrell, and executive produced the independent film *The TV Set*, a scathingly funny look at the television industry starring David Duchovny and Sigourney Weaver. Prior to that, he produced the hit DreamWorks comedy *Anchorman: The Legend of Ron Burgundy*, also starring Ferrell, Christina Applegate, and Paul Rudd.

He served as an executive producer of the critically praised, award-winning television series *Freaks and Geeks*, which debuted in the 1999–2000 season. He also wrote and directed several episodes of the series, which still maintains a following and was recently released on DVD. He also created and executive-produced the series *Undeclared*, just released on video. *Undeclared*, about college freshmen, was named one of *Time* magazine's Ten Best Shows of 2001.

Apatow previously worked as a writer, director, and producer on the award-winning and widely acclaimed series *The Larry Sanders Show*, starring Garry Shandling. For his work on the show, he earned an Emmy nomination for Outstanding Writing for a Comedy Series and received five consecutive Emmy Award nominations for Outstanding Comedy Series. In addition, *The Larry Sanders Show* brought Apatow two Cable ACE Awards for Best Comedy Series and a Writers Guild of America Award nomination.

SHAUNA ROBERTSON (Producer) recently produced *Forgetting Sarah Marshall* for Universal in Hawaii, starring Jason Segel, Mila Kunis, Kristen Bell, and Russell Brand, and *Pineapple Express* for Sony. Written by Seth Rogen & Evan Goldberg, this film is directed by David Gordon Green and stars Rogen, James Franco, and Danny McBride. Other credits include *Knocked Up* with writer-director-producer Judd Apatow for Universal pictures, starring Seth Rogen, Katherine Heigl, Leslie Mann, and Paul Rudd; *The 40-Year-Old Virgin*; *Anchorman: The Legend of Ron Burgundy*; and *Elf*, directed by Jon Favreau.

She also served as a co-producer on Jay Roach's *Meet the Parents*, starring Ben Stiller and Robert De Niro. In 1997, Robertson partnered with Roach to form Everyman Pictures and worked on such notable film projects as *Austin Powers: International Man of Mystery* and its sequel *Austin Powers: The Spy Who Shagged Me*, as well as *Mystery, Alaska*, and the adaptation of Douglas Adams' novel *The Hitchhiker's Guide to the Galaxy*.

Superbad

Acknowledgments

We wish to thank the following for their special contributions to the book:

At Apatow Films: Seth Rogen and Evan Goldberg, David Goldberg, Judd Apatow, Matt Bass, Andrew Epstein, and Lisa Yadavaia.

At Sony Pictures Entertainment: George Leon, Juli Boylan, Greg Economos, Mark Caplan, Cindy Irwin, Ashley Maidy, and Kristy Chang.

Special thanks to Timothy Shaner at Night & Day Design (nightanddaydesign.biz) and to the Newmarket team, including Frank DeMaio, Paul Sugarman, Linda Carbone, Haley Pierson, Melissa Heller, Heidi Sachner, Harry Burton, and Tracey Bussell.

—Esther Margolis, Publisher, and Keith Hollaman, Executive Editor, Newmarket Press

Evan   Seth

Credits

PHOTOGRAPHY: All unit photography by Melissa Moseley, except the photograph on page 6 by Eric Charbonneau © 2007 WireImage.com. Used by permission.

Permission to reprint copyrighted material from the following sources is gratefully acknowledged. The publisher has made every effort to contact copyright holders; any errors or omissions are inadvertent and will be corrected upon notice in future reprintings.

PAGE 23: "The Boys of Summer," by David Edelstein, August 27, 2007. Reprinted with permission by *New York* magazine. Copyright © 2007 by *New York* magazine.

PAGE 26: Review by Peter Travers from *Rolling Stone*, August 7, 2007 © Rolling Stone LLC 2007. All rights reserved. Reprinted by permission.

PAGE 29: "It's, Like, a Buddy Film by, Like, Buddies," by Michael Cieply, August 5, 2007. From *The New York Times*, August 5, 2007 © 2007 *The New York Times*. All rights reserved.

PAGE 33: "Talkin' Superbad: Comedy Isn't Pretty," by Josh Rottenberg, August 17, 2007. Copyright Entertainment Weekly Inc. Reprinted by permission. *Entertainment Weekly* is a registered trademark of Entertainment Weekly Inc. All rights reserved.

PAGE 104: Lyrics from "Black Water" by Patrick Simmons © 1974 (Renewed) WB Music Corp. (ASCAP) All rights administered by WB Music Corp. All rights reserved.